Transpacific Imaginations

History, Literature, Counterpoetics

Yunte Huang

HARVARD UNIVERSITY PRESS

Cambridge, Massachusetts

London, England

2008

Library of Congress Cataloging-in-Publication Data

Huang, Yunte.
  Transpacific imaginations : history, literature, counterpoetics /
Yunte Huang.
       p.   cm.
  Includes bibliographical references and index.
  ISBN-13: 978-0-674-02637-7 (alk. paper)
  ISBN-10: 0-674-02637-3 (alk. paper)
     1. American literature—Asian influences.   2. American literature—19th
  century—History and criticism.   3. American literature—20th century—
  History and criticism.   4. American literature—Asian American authors—
  History and criticism.   5. Pacific Area—In literature.   I. Title.
  PS159.A85H83   2007
  810.9'325—dc22   2007020027

*For Isabelle Huang
and Ira Huang*

Contents

Acknowledgments

I started this book project in New England and finished it on the Pacific coast. Such geographical facts are stated here not for their autobiographical value, but for their relevance to one of my central concerns in this book: the situatedness of imagination. Contrary to its romantic claim to transcendence, imagination, as I have learned from my study as well as from my own trajectory as an intellectual migrant, is situated in, if not simply bound to, a particular location or standpoint of the imaginer.

When I arrived in Cambridge, Massachusetts, in the fall of 1999 to start my first academic job as an assistant professor of English at Harvard, I had just finished a dissertation, later turned into a book, on what I call the transpacific migrations of cultural meanings through the work of poetry and translation. I was interested in the ways in which poems, narratives, stories, and other kinds of literary artifacts or motifs manage to break through cultural, linguistic boundaries and transform themselves in their ever displaced settlements. By focusing on cross-cultural poetics, I tried to make a point that the book was less about the migrations of people than about the migrations of texts. Part of me is still deeply committed to such language-based mobility studies, but the four years at Harvard have also taught me that imagination is not just a supreme fiction riding on the wings of poesy and that people, even with their best intentions, cannot escape the human or institutional situations from which their imaginative flights are set to take off.

Since in the current book I am writing about the kind of American imperial imaginary that originated in New England (via Emerson, Melville, Adams, and so on) and came to clash with other kinds of imaginaries in the Pacific, the geographical location of the launching point of my book project seems to carry some real as well as symbolic meanings. The same goes for my eventual escape from the cultural powerhouse in New England and finishing the book on the Pacific coast, where there seems to be no glass ceiling and the blue sky appears to be the only limit.

This line of flight of mine, however, is hardly original. Throughout this journey I have been fortunate to be able to count many as my predecessors and fellow travelers. Among them I want to specify at least two, whose thinking and writing about unsettling in the wilderness of American history and poetry have provided me great sources of inspiration: Susan Howe and Rob Wilson. I first came to know Susan when I was still a graduate student in Buffalo. But our intellectual friendship flowered after I moved to Cambridge, where she had grown up. Daughter of a famous Harvard law professor and an Irish American novelist, Susan has always been both at the center and margin of American culture. Her deep knowledge of all the eccentricities of colonial New England has given me a rare glimpse into the inner workings of a culture to which I am an outsider, and her fiercely independent scholarship, long marginalized by mainstream academia until recently, has taught me both a sense of awe in the face of powerful cultural institutions and a spirit of rebellion against them. In the long summer of 2001, while I was working on the Melville part of my book, Susan would often drive up from Guilford to Cambridge and do research at the Houghton Library for her now published book, *The Midnight*. We spent many hours sitting at teahouses, cafes, and restaurants, chatting about our shared interests in antiquarianism, books, marginalia, handwriting, ghosts, and so on. Through her work and her personal influence, Susan has showed me the walls of American cultural institutions, the cracks in them, as well as giving me a chisel to dig.

Like Susan, Rob is also a New Englander turning against the colonial, imperialist legacy of New England culture. Born in what he ironically calls Connect-i-cut, Rob has become a "Pacific man," living first in the Bay Area, then many years in Hawaii, and now back in Santa Cruz. His trademark "mongrel poetics," a fascinating mixture of New Age beatitude, local Pacific experimentalism, and global soul searching, has showed me that the flight to the West is not just an interpretive dance in the blind spot of Emersonian Transcendentalism, nor merely a poke in the "transparent eyeball," but instead an active worlding that reclaims history and geography back from the imperial sublimes. Rob's candid critique of the text-based materialism of my earlier writings has much to do with some of the new directions the current book is taking. For that as well as for his invaluable advice and help over the years, I remain truly grateful.

I also wish to thank my editor at the Harvard University Press, Lindsay Waters, for his unfailing faith in my work and his patient guidance throughout the process of writing and finishing up the book. It has been my fortune to have an editor who, as a critic and thinker himself, shares my interests in the transpacific issues. I also want to thank Phoebe Kosman for her superb editorial assistance. I am also grateful to the three anonymous readers for the press as well as Juliana Spahr for having reviewed the manuscript with such care and insight; they have made this a much better book.

Colleagues and friends who have read parts of the manuscript or heard my presentations and have provided thoughts and suggestions include Hank Lazer, Lawrence Buell, Donald Pease, Charles Bernstein, Marjorie Perloff, Giles Gunn, Rita Raley, Mark Rose, Jennifer Salen, and Jerome Rothenberg.

Part of the Conclusion appeared as a short essay in *Comparative Literature* 57:3 (2005).

Grateful acknowledgment is given to the University of Washington Press for permission to reprint poems from Him Mark Lai, Genny Lim, and Judy Yung, *Island: Poetry and History of Chinese Immigrants on Angel Island, 1910–1940* (Copyright © 1980 by the HOC DOI Project); to the University of California Press for permission to reprint from Theresa Cha, *Dictee* (Copyright © 2001 by the Regents of the University of California); to Coffee House Press and Lawson Fusao Inada for permission to reprint from Lawson Fusao Inada, *Legends from Camp* (Copyright © 1993 by Lawson Fusao Inada); to the Segue Foundation and Kent Johnson for permission to use material from Araki Yasusada, *Doubled Flowering* (Copyright © 1997 by Kent Johnson); and to Joan Myers for permission to use her photograph "Jerome Smokestack."

No longer THINGS but what happens BETWEEN things, these are the terms of the reality contemporary to us.

—Charles Olson

When man truly approaches the Other he is uprooted from history.

—Emmanuel Levinas

Introduction: The Transpacific as a Critical Space

In the early days of my research and writing that have led to the current book, whenever my American colleagues asked me what I meant by the "transpacific imagination," I would use *Moby-Dick* as an example. I would tell them that Herman Melville was what Charles Olson called the "Pacific Man," someone who has crossed the line of horizon; that the book, besides what generations of Melville scholars have made it out to be, is a profound meditation on the destiny of the Pacific in the context of U.S. imperial history; and that for me as a writer who has also gone across the Pacific, Melville's book traces an imaginary line of flight from homogeneous visions, be they national, cultural, historical, or literary.[1]

Somewhere in the middle of my explanation, a question would pop up; my interlocutor would stop me by asking, "But isn't *Moby-Dick* set in the Atlantic?" At first I was both annoyed and amused, but I soon realized that their not knowing the geographical setting for one of the most commonly read books in American literature classes was a symptom of something larger than personal gaps of knowledge (most of my colleagues are literary professionals). To be more specific, their confusion was a result of decades of canonical symbolist readings (from F. O. Matthiessen to Lawrance Thompson, Charles Feidelson, Jr., James L. Guetti, T. Walker Herbert, Jr., Bainard Cowan, and so on) of this American classic, readings that see the book as merely an allegory (for the battle between good and evil, democracy versus autocracy, capitalism versus communism, and so on) and shun the geopolitics lying at the heart of Melville's concern.[2]

My own study of *Moby-Dick* follows an alternative, geopolitically conscious line of thinking that tries to unsettle symbol-minded readings of this and other canonical American literary texts. Starting with Charles Olson, scholars such as Stephen H. Sumida, William Spanos, John Carlos Rowe, Amy Kaplan, David Palumbo-Liu, and Rob Wilson have tried to situate American literature against the background of the United States as a Pacific empire.[3] Likewise, I use the phrase "transpacific imaginations" to refer to a host of literary and historical imaginations that have emerged under the tremendous geopolitical pressure of the Pacific encounters. My central concern is with the possibilities of literary representation and historical knowledge in the transpacific context. Through readings of an array of authors and texts that are usually not read together in any national literary history, I seek to uncover a critical terrain that Melville has called "the deadly space between." It is both a contact zone between competing geopolitical ambitions and a gap between literature and history that is riddled with distortions, half-truths, longings, and affective burdens never fully resolved in the unevenly temporalized space of the transpacific.

"The Deadly Space Between"

Melville took the "deadly" phrase from the Scottish poet Thomas Campbell's "The Battle of the Baltic" (1809):

> But the might of England flush'd
> To anticipate the scene;
> And her van the fleeter rush'd
> O'er the deadly space between.[4]

A popular English war song throughout the nineteenth century, Campbell's ballad depicts a crucial battle between the English and the Danish fleets near Copenhagen in 1801; "the deadly space between" refers to the perilous strip of water in the Baltic that momentarily divides the enemies. As Melville was keenly aware, this phrase would be an equally apt description of another perilous body of water, namely, the Pacific, which bore witness to the deadliest battles in modern times in the same way the Baltic did to the wars of the old empires. In "Billy Budd," Melville turns the phrase into a metaphor for the insurmountable distance between a normal human nature and a villain's evil character. The insurmountability lies, as Melville indicates, less in the actual length of the distance than in the deadly inadequacy of human language to measure the gap. For words to attempt to adequately address the "irritating juxtaposition" of the satanic Claggart and the Christ-like Billy Budd would be to force language to tread in treacherous, "deadly" waters, like the Pacific.[5]

Melville's metaphoric use of Campbell's phrase, charged with sedimentations of transatlantic imperial memory, has proven to be both an obstacle and inspiration for me as I enter the discursive terrain of the transpacific. Obstacle, because Melville's metaphorism is an open invitation to the canonical symbolist elision of the transpacific in his work. Inspiration, because his resort to metaphorism exemplifies not only the deadliness of the geopolitical reality that constantly escapes the grasp of language, but also the slipperiness and ambiguity of the space between the two discursive modes in the subtitle of my book—history and literature. Exploring the fault lines of historical and literary imaginations across the Pacific, I want to show that the gap between the historical and the literary, between the documentary and the fictional, may be crossed over only at one's own peril. Or, as Melville suggests, the crossing, if attempted at all, is best "by indirection" (324), a path paved with literary devices, inventions, or, simply, fictions. This is the path my book attempts to tread on, one that will lead to both historical fictions and literary truths of the transpacific imaginary.

I use "fiction" and "truth" in their plurals in order to suggest that I am dealing with different or differentiated histories here. I do not mean simply that each Pacific nation, culture, or island—the United States, China, Japan, Korea, the Philippines, Hawaii, Tahiti, and so on—has distinct memories of the past. What concerns me rather is the different ways of enunciating the past and projecting the future with respect to a distinct sense of historicity. As Robert Borofsky reminds us in his groundbreaking anthology of writings on the "pasts" of the Pacific, "Different people make sense of the past in different ways. To assert the past has a single, fixed, interpretation—that everyone concurs on through time—is to rob it of the one thing we can be certain about, the past's contingent, negotiated, changing nature."[6]

In other words, histories are different not simply because they have separate stories to tell, but because they have, to use Claude Lévi-Strauss's term, different temporalities.[7] Temporality is a relation to time that is by nature unevenly punctured, or, to use a tautology, temporalized. As the relation to time becomes increasingly homogenized in the age of globalization, the notion of historical difference has often been watered down to fact-finding through the lens of a common measure. But as Louis Althusser puts it in his famous attack on Hegelian historiography, it is impossible "to think the process of the different levels of the whole in the same historical time. Each of these different 'levels' does not have the same type of historical existence . . . Each of these peculiar histories is punctuated with peculiar rhythms and can only be known on condition that we have defined the concept of the specificity of its historical temporality and its punctuations."[8]

The implications of the transpacific as "the deadly space between" are thus twofold: one pertains to the combat zone between History and histories, and the other the gap between history and literature. Obviously, the first use is historical or literal because it describes wars of discourses on the destiny of the Pacific; and the second use is literary or metaphoric because in this case the transpacific provides a backdrop for my contemplations on the epistemological battle between the documentary and the fictional. One may say, then, that this book on the transpacific as a deadly in-between contains a deadly gap in itself.

My answer to such a charge is also twofold. First, in the long history of the colonization of the Pacific, (this) space has always been conceived by the colonizers both literally and abstractly—literally as objects for territorial expansion and abstractly as typological fulfillment. As this book will show, such a double vision of the Pacific—one in which material possession and discursive abstraction reinforce each other—remains the central legacy of Pacific history/historiography. By looking at the transpacific as both a terrain of geopolitical struggle and an instance of epistemological battle, I mean to tackle that legacy head on and revision that double vision. Second, "counterpoetics," the third term in my subtitle, carries on the critique of the violence of the imperial double vision. I use counterpoetics to describe a host of marginalized poetic/historiographical practices: antiquarianism, collection, local history, anecdotes, family genealogy, travel writing, graffiti, correspondence, fantasies, and hoaxes. As a counterpoint to imperial visions that always claim some version of historical teleology as their raison d'être, such poetics hovers between the literal and the metaphoric, the historical and the mimetic. And in contrast to the master narratives, these works of counterpoetics turn away from any meta-discourse on the transpacific; they move instead toward the enactment of poetic imagination as a means to alter memory and invoke minority survival in the deadly space between competing national, imperial interests and between authoritative regimes of epistemology serving those interests. The conceptual gap between the transpacific as the geopolitical and the metaphoric may not, therefore, be bridged or abridged—a Melvillean curse/blessing. Instead, as I will propose in the conclusion to this book, the transpacific lesson is one of learning to live in or with the gap in the spirit of a hermeneutics of recognition and acknowledgment, called for in part by the works of counterpoetics.

The Critical Space

In his monumental study of spatial production, Henri Lefebvre analyzes four kinds of social space: absolute, abstract, contradictory, and differential. Absolute space, according to Lefebvre, is made up of fragments of nature located at sites that are chosen for their intrinsic qualities but whose consecration stripped them of their natural characteristics and uniqueness.[9] Agropastoral in origin, such space corresponds to the precapitalist mode of production and is "lived" rather than conceived. It is a representational space rather than a representation of space; no sooner is it conceptualized than its significance wanes and vanishes and absolute space becomes abstract space (236). In its Euclidean geometric, optical, or phallic formant, abstract space is a product of violence of war and "serves those forces which make a *tabula rasa* of whatever stands in their way, of whatever threatens them—in short, of differences. These forces seem to grind down and crush everything before them, with space performing the function of a plane, a bulldozer or a tank" (285). Homogeneous as it seems, abstract space is filled with contradictions (quantity versus quality, production versus consumption, global versus fragmentary, exchange value versus use value, knowledge versus power, understanding versus violence, etc.) and is thus essentially a contradictory space (352–358). The components in this abstract/contradictory space are particularities that confront one another and clash with one another. "Out of their struggles, which imply and complicate class struggles as well as conflicts between peoples and nations, there emerge differences properly so called"; hence we find the fourth term, differential space (373).

As seen through Lefebvre's critical lens, the Pacific also needs to be understood in multilayered ways, simultaneously as an absolute, abstract, contradictory, and differential space. As I show in Part One, by following the spatial and discursive trajectories of three transpacific travelers, Mark Twain, Henry Adams, and Liang Qichao, the Pacific needs to be viewed from different shores. As Twain and Adams were well aware, the territorial expansion into the Pacific in the nineteenth century was not only an extension of America's Manifest Destiny, but also a step in the historical progression of the world. As the Puritan typology would have it, the center of the world moves from the Mediterranean to the Atlantic and now to the Pacific. But as Liang came to realize painfully, turn-of-the-century China's inability to compete with other nations in the Pacific signaled the bankruptcy of traditional Confucian historiography and the end of the eternally cyclical time spatialized in the boundlessness of the Middle Kingdom. The Pacific is the dead end of historical thinking for premodern China, whereas it is a new manifestation of providential design for the United States. Thus, the discourse of the Pacific Century, the notion of the Pacific as the new center of the world, ushering all nations into the last stage of Universal History, necessarily camouflages the fissures and wounds opened up by the clashes between these differentiated histories.

In *The Clash of Empires,* Lydia H. Liu reminds us that the battle of words and translations is central to the sovereign will that had driven the wars between empires. The title of Liu's book is meant to be a corrective to Samuel P. Huntington's theory of "clash of civilizations." "Civilizations don't clash," Liu states resolutely, "but empires do." In contrast to Huntington's interpretation of world conflicts as results of competitions among monolithic, homogeneous blocks of civilizations, Liu describes a world in which signs and meanings are in constant circulation, exchange, and reinvestment.[10] Sharing Liu's belief in the significance of word battles, I intend in this book to study the clash not of civilizations or of empires, but of discourses. To be specific, my interest lies in looking at the transpacific as a space in which the destiny of the Pacific is subject to competing interpretations made from different shores.

Imagination; or, Its Transpacific Fallout

Moby-Dick; or, The Whale, which I treat extensively in Part Two, is a poetic enactment of the breakdown of a particular kind of transpacific imagination as advocated by Emerson and other spokespersons for the nineteenth-century U.S. imperial vision. The correlation between Emersonian transcendentalism and U.S. imperial, capitalist expansion has been fruitfully explored by recent scholars.[11] My study, via Melville, is intended to look at the geo-specific manifestations of the imperial vision and the ultimate failure of such transpacific imagination.

Samuel Taylor Coleridge defines imagination as "a repetition in the infinite mind of the eternal act of creation in the infinite I AM."[12] In "Nature," Emerson turns Romanticist imagination into an engine of self-sublimation and individual autonomy: "Standing on the bare ground,—my head bathed by the blithe air, and uplifted into infinite space,—all mean egotism vanishes. I become a transparent eye-ball. I am nothing. I see all. The currents of the Universal Being circulate through me; I am part or particle of God."[13] The ideological consequence of such a transcendental eyeballing is the elision of space and people in nature. "Vast spaces of nature," Emerson writes in "Self-Reliance," "the Atlantic Ocean, the South Sea,—long intervals of time, years, centuries,— are of no account."[14] As Wilson points out, Emerson's sublime transcendence is achieved by mastering Atlantic and Pacific spaces and people into ciphers and turning history into a diary of national (and private) self-empowerment.[15]

It is against such a grain of imperial imagination that Melville, who famously refuses to see things as mere "ciphers," writes *Moby-Dick* as a transpacific book. Rather than imagination, the paradigm that Melville follows, I argue, is "collection" with its various manifestations in the fields of economy, literature, and history just at the time when the United States was emerging as a new Pacific empire. In economic terms, as I explain in Part Two, the collecting of natural resources in the Pacific, including whales, furs, bêches-de-mer, tortoiseshell, pearls, shark fins, spices, human heads, and human beings, served vital economic interests to the United States in the nineteenth century. But Melville is deeply interested in collecting also for its subversive, antiprogressive potentials. The ambivalence of collecting as primitive accumulation for capitalist production and as an antiquarian obsession thwarting production thus provides a backdrop for my engagement with Ahab, Ishmael, Queequeg, and finally, Melville himself, as collectors who hover in the abyss of conflicting economic interests. Ahab, for instance, instead of acting as a cool-headed industrial manager who steers the ship toward the pursuit of commodities—ordinary whales—for their exchange values, becomes a monomaniac collector who is obsessed with a single collectible item—Moby Dick—for the sake of its nonexchangeable aura. His collector's appreciation for singularity thus leads him to change the course of the *Pequod* and eventually run it aground, ruining a transpacific pursuit of economic interests.

Collection as a subversive economic practice, one in which a collector arranges the collectibles into a magic circle and keeps them out of the system of exchangeability, finds literary and historiographical ramifications in a reader reading a text in an antihermeneutic manner, a writer assembling words as objects into a text as collection, and an antiquarianist historian living closely to his multitudinous details and rejecting luminous abstractions. In a society like the nineteenth-century United States, which prefers exchange, abstraction, and progress to use, singularity, and stasis, the sinking of a whaling ship by a whale, the pursuer by the pursued, becomes a powerful anticlimax in the drama the new Pacific empire has just begun to stage by mobilizing all the arsenals in its historical, economic, and literary imagination: the Pacific as the "final frontier" in Universal History, as the future of American economy, and as the setting for Western romance fiction with its predetermined narrative closure.

Imagination; or, Its Counterpoetic Work

But the Pacific can be imagined very differently, and imagination itself may do different kinds of cultural work if mobilized outside of the Emersonian, Romanticist perimeter. When asked why the Pacific attracts him, James Clifford, a leading postmodern thinker, says, "For me the Pacific has a special clarity. In a strange way, Papua New Guinea, Vanuatu, and such places are in a kind of time warp. Everyone knows the Pacific's 'out there', 'back then',—never seen as modern. I actually think that is one of its great advantages, as it were, to think with. Once one takes it out of its past tense and places it in a contemporary context, it becomes possible to see its stories, its narratives, its history and historical change as only tenuously linked to linear modernist histories of progress and development. It becomes possible to see what I might call aprogressive narratives of modernity. It is both politically and empirically quite important to think about these types of narratives."[16]

It is in the spirit of looking for such "aprogressive narratives" that I have set out, in Part Three, to explore imaginations that resist narrative closure and historical teleology as enunciated and projected in the transpacific space. In the case of Angel Island poetry (Chapter 9), the counterpoetics is manifested in *tibishi* ("poetry inscribed on the wall") as a mode of inscription that sits uneasily with literary and historical authority. Written on the walls of the detaining station for Chinese immigrants, these poems delineate alternative modes of spatial and temporal practice whose subversive poetics would elude us if we treated them merely as a historical record of transpacific displacements of people. In my reading, these poems perform the cultural politics of protest literature associated with the simultaneously condemned and condoned form of urban graffiti. Also, as a Chinese genre of travel writing, these poems on the wall constitute an important outlet for the politically powerless to address historical issues when the conventional form of historical writing is strictly prohibited without authorization.

In the subsequent two chapters I continue to explore poetic resistance to imperial, national, and other forms of homogeneous narratives of the transpacific. As I argue in Chapter 10, if Angel Island represents modern America's attempt to manage its racial frontier along the Pacific, the internment of Japanese Americans during World War II may also be understood as a spatial practice of dissecting America's transpacific routes through a racialized reterritorialization. In this regard, I see the poetry of Lawson Fusao Inada as an instance of countering the production of what Lefebvre would call abstract space by the imperial state power. Chapter 11 further complicates the traditional paradigm of conceiving the transpacific as an oppositional space of the East versus the West, Asia versus America. Addressing Japan's occupation of Korea as a case of internal colonization within the East Asian region, Theresa Cha's *Dictee* is concerned with poetry as a testimony, not document, of colonial history and violence.

In these works of counterpoetics, imagination departs from its Romanticist, transcendentalist origin and spreads new roots in "articulation" as a situated and contested social imaginary. In the idiosyncratically mongrel poetic language of Wilson, imagination becomes "an act of semi-joyous signifying that both props up ('Structures') and distorts ('masks') the materials of social reality, and works (through the production of some symbolic 'excess' to cover up the holes) to conceal and reveal (via sublimation, displacement, and other defenses) those social traumas and antagonisms haunting its very creation."[17] Writing against colonial violence, historical traumas, and narrative closures as the centerpieces of transpacific history, the authors I study in Part Three have mobilized imagination, not as the faculty of a gifted individual, but as a collective imaginary that, as Arjun Appadurai has argued, both consolidates and threatens ideas of community, locality, ethnicity, and nationality.[18]

But these poetic subversions stand in a tantalizing relation to the case of hoax or forgery studied in the Conclusion. In the scandal of *Doubled Flowering,* English readers were tricked into believing that they were reading gripping accounts of the horror of the Hiroshima bombing by a dying survivor, Araki Yasusada, only to realize later that these poems and the poetic personae were fabricated by a white American poet who had been discontented with the recent flowering of ethnic, minority writings. This shadow-play of history, which feeds on the American legacy of guilt in the wake of the bombing, mocks our attempt to valorize those poetic subversions we have so much cherished. Thus, we are forced to look back again, over this unfathomable chasm filled with perilous water, to see if we still stand on treacherous and deadly ground. Rejecting the false dichotomy between the East and the West, between (their) history and (our) literature, as implied in the case of Yasusada, I propose a poetics of acknowledgment as a way to reimagine the transpacific. Only by means of acknowledgment rather than knowledge, through recognition of both the ontological status of the Other and the epistemological gaps in our knowledge, can we begin to approach the conditions of collective responsibility and planetary imagination.

PART ONE

History:
And the Views from the Shores

The phrase "And the Views from the Shores" is meant to echo, with small variations, the title of a book by Stephen H. Sumida.[1] In his attempt to recover and re-envision a local and localized literary tradition, Sumida uses the title phrase, "And the View from the Shore," as a dialogical rebuke to views of the Pacific islands typically from a departing cruise ship, in the midst of aloha music and hula dance. The plurals in my paraphrase, however, are meant to suggest that the transpacific space may be lived, conceptualized from multiple, contested points of origin. As Rob Wilson reminds us, "The Pacific remains a multiple region, to be sure, defying Western categorization or easy framing into any national trajectory."[2] Or, as Arif Dirlik puts it, "There is no Pacific region that is an 'objective' given, but only a competing set of ideational constructs that project upon a certain location on the globe the imperatives of interest, power or vision of these historically produced relationships."[3] In this part of my book, by following the transpacific trajectories of Mark Twain, Henry Adams, and Liang Qichao, I want to show how the emerging discourses of the Pacific have produced a transnational, transoceanic space that is unevenly temporalized.

Demonstrating the multiplicity of views from the shores or otherwise is not, however, my ultimate goal here. The transpacific space may indeed be experienced and represented in multilayered ways as Henri Lefebvre has suggested, but the transpacific multiplicity must be understood from a more critical, not merely descriptive, lens.[4] Hence, the real stress in my phrase, "And the views from the shores," falls on the first, conjunctive word, "and." Almost Poundian in its poetic, anti-epic effect, "and" is, in the words of Gilles Deleuze and Claire Parnet, "neither a union, nor a juxtaposition, but the birth of a stammering, the outline of a broken line."[5] Rather than a signifier for spatial contiguity or temporal continuity, "and" is a "between," or a "deadly space between." In their somewhat romanticized view of what they call "the superiority of Anglo-American literature" (in contrast to continent-bound European literature), Deleuze and Parnet believe that Anglo-American literature has created an "and" as a line of flight to replace the continental concern with Being: "Substitute the AND for IS. A *and* B. The AND is not even a specific relation or conjunction, it is that which subtends all relations, the path of all relations, which makes relations shoot outside their terms and outside the set of their terms, and outside everything which could be determined as Being, One, Whole. The AND as extra-being, inter-being."[6] In this book, I want to suggest that the *and-* effect and its ideological consequences may be felt and realized not within the perimeter of Anglo-American literature and culture but outside it. The transpacific, in other words, becomes such a paratactic AND, which critically undermines all appropriative discourses that rely on the definitive formulas of "The Pacific IS . . .": "The Pacific is the final frontier," "The Pacific is an American lake," "The Pacific is the dead end of Chinese history," *and* so on.

1

Mark Twain:
Letters from Hawaii

The loveliest fleet of islands that lies anchored in any ocean.

—Mark Twain

On March 18, 1866, the *Ajax,* a newly inaugurated steamer service between San Francisco and Hawaii, brought to the Sandwich islands a fledgling American writer who had just adopted the pseudonym "Mark Twain." He had traveled widely in the American West but had not published any book. He was now commissioned by the Sacramento *Union,* a leading newspaper in the region, to spend a month in the islands as a traveling correspondent. The twenty-five picturesque letters he would write from Hawaii to be published in the newspaper were not just fulfillments of his commission, but constituted an important step in his writing career. Some years later, when writing his book of western travel, *Roughing It* (1872), Mark Twain incorporated these Hawaiian letters into the book. In 1884 he began to write a novel with a Hawaiian setting. Although the manuscript of that book (except for the seventeen pages now in the collection at the library of the University of California at Berkeley) has not survived, Twain incorporated much of the material into a novel with a different setting—*A Connecticut Yankee in King Arthur's Court* (1889). His later travelogue, *Following the Equator* (1897), retraces his earlier footsteps on the islands and modifies his earlier views on America's Manifest Destiny in the Pacific.

In these letters, Twain draws a clear picture of the capitalist expansion into the future fiftieth state of the United States. He describes in detail the sugar and whaling industries, which were of great interest to American businessmen (who are the intended readers of the newspaper), as well as the Hawaiian trade, whose exports bring high fees to the U.S. Customs. Twain documents meticulously the benefits the Hawaiian islands can bring to the U.S. economy, including natural resources, products, trade, and human resources. He advocates recruiting coolies from China and using them in Hawaiian sugarcane plantations, California mines, manufacturing businesses, and public improvement corporations (railroad building). In letter 23, Twain writes, "You will not always go on paying $80 and $100 a month for labor which you can hire for $5. The sooner California adopts coolie labor the better it will be for her."[1] And he prophesies the fabulous future of California and the Pacific, hailing the trade route to Hawaii as the long-looked for Northwest Passage to the East:

> To America it has been vouchsafed to materialize the vision, and realize the dream of centuries, of the enthusiasts of the Old World. We have found the true Northwest Passage—we have found the true and only direct route to the bursting coffers of "Ormus and of Ind"—to the enchanted land whose mere drippings, in the ages that are gone, enriched and aggrandized ancient Venice, first, then Portugal, Holland, and in our own time, England—and each in succession they longed and sought for the fountainhead of this vast Oriental wealth, and sought in vain. The path was hidden to them, but we have found it over the waves of the Pacific, and American enterprise will penetrate to the heart and center of its hoarded treasures, its imperial affluence. (274)

The letters give a sure sign of the mercantile purpose of Twain's propagating the cause of the American Pacific: though Twain documents in great detail the islands' scenery and climate, politics, social conditions, history and legends, and so on, he makes no mention of leprosy, a disease brought into the kingdom of Hawaii before 1854. He probably does not wish to frighten off the businessmen who will be reading his letters with an eye on possible trade trips.

But these Hawaiian letters go far beyond the purpose of economic advocacy. As the above quote indicates, Twain understands the Hawaiian issue with a deep sense of history. Unlike Henry Adams, whose transpacific voyage we will study next, Twain has done extensive research by reading histories, studying lexicon and phrase books, examining newspapers and government documents, and learning Hawaiian mythology and traditions.[2] Through these complex layers of textual, historical traces, Twain discovers, not easily graspable truths, but ever conflicting conceptions and perceptions of events that have unfolded on the watery stage of the Pacific. What particularly draws Twain's attention is the story about Captain Cook.

Cook's apotheosis has long been a controversy in Pacific historiography. Even today, historians and anthropologists are divided on the issue, both intellectually and ideologically.[3] The questions surrounding the apotheosis are as factual as they are interpretive and political: Did the natives actually believe that Cook was their long-awaited god Lono? To what extent did Cook willingly participate in the cross-cultural misrecognition? How did he die, or what eventually sealed his doom? Picking his way through the maze of historical traces, Twain relies mostly on American missionary, anti-British versions of Hawaiian history, which debunks the myth of Cook. "Plain unvarnished history takes the romance out of Captain Cook's assassination," writes Twain in letter 19, "and renders a deliberate verdict of justifiable homicide. Wherever he went among the islands he was cordially received and welcomed by the inhabitants, and his ships lavishly supplied with all manner of food. He returned these kindnesses with insult and ill-treatment" (215). Despite Twain's rhetorical claim that he has access to "plain unvarnished history," his letters reveal that he is fully aware of the palimpsestic nature of historical narratives and the irreconcilability of conflicting views.

Among the Cook relics he has discovered on the islands, there is a heavily inscribed tree stump to which Twain will now add his own layer of inscription:

> Tramping about in the rear of the warehouse, we suddenly came upon another object of interest. It was a coconut stump, four or five feet high, and about a foot in diameter at the butt. It had lava bowlders piled around its base to hold it up and keep it in its place, and it was entirely sheathed over, from top to bottom, with rough, discolored sheets of copper, such as ships' bottoms are coppered with. Each sheet had a rude inscription scratched upon it—with a nail, apparently—and in every case the execution was wretched. It was almost dark by this time, and the inscriptions would have been difficult to read even at noonday, but with patience and industry I finally got them all in my note-book. They read as follows:
>
> "Near this spot fell CAPTAIN JAMES COOK, The Distinguished Circumnavigator who Discovered these islands A.D. 1778. His Majesty's Ship Imogene, October 17, 1837."
>
> "Parties from H. M. ship Vixen visited this spot Jan. 25, 1858."
>
> "This sheet and capping put on by Sparrowhawk, September 16, 1839, in order to preserve this monument to the memory of Cook."
>
> "Captain Montressor and officers of H.M.S. Calypso visited this spot the 18th of October, 1858."

> "This tree having fallen, was replaced on this spot by H.M.S.V. Cor-
> morant, G. T. Gordon, Esq., Captain, who visited this bay May 18, 1846."
> "This bay was visited, July 4, 1843, by H.M.S. Carysfort, the Right Hon-
> orable Lord George Paulet, Captain, to whom, as the representative of Her
> Britannic Majesty Queen Victoria, these islands were ceded, February 25,
> 1843." (223–224)

These graffiti-like carvings on a tree stump are attempts by captains of
visiting ships to commemorate Cook's death. Oddly enough, the stump
had first been created by a cannon ball, a symbol of colonial violence:
"After Cook's murder, his second in command, on board the ship,
opened fire upon the swarms of natives on the beach, and one of his
cannon balls cut this coconut tree short off and left this monumental
stump standing" (224). There is another monument, or sort of, that
competes with the stump for Twain's attention:

> up on the mountain side we had passed by a large inclosure like an
> ample hog-pen, built of lava blocks, which marks the spot where
> Cook's flesh was stripped from his bones and burned; but this is not
> properly a monument, since it was erected by the natives themselves,
> and less to do honor to the circumnavigator than for the sake of conve-
> nience in roasting him. (Ibid.)

Black humor aside, Twain's description acknowledges that for the events
taking place in the Pacific, there are always different monuments,
different perceptions, and different interpretations. The ship captains'
inscriptions restage the apotheosis of Cook, this time as a Western hero;
but the natives' hog-pen, as a quasi-monument, reveals the earthly nature of a man whom they had once taken for their god.

Such perceptual differences with regard to events, objects, and beings
dominate the history of Pacific encounters. As Twain continues to explore these differences, he becomes increasingly critical of Cook for his
nonchalance toward native cultural artifacts while exploiting their cultural beliefs. Twain quotes from his source,

> "On the 2d of February, at the desire of his commander, Captain King
> proposed to the priests to purchase for fuel the railing which sur-
> rounded the top of the temple of Lono!" . . . Cook desecrated the holy
> places of the temple by storing supplies for his ships in them, and by
> using the level grounds within the enclosures as a general workshop
> for repairing his sails, etc.—ground which was so sacred that no

common native dared to set his foot upon it . . . Two iron hatches were offered for the temple railing, and when the sacrilegious proposition was refused by the priests with horror and indignation, it was torn down by order of Captain Cook and taken to the boats by the sailors, and the images which surrounded it removed and destroyed in the presence of the priests and chiefs. (218–219)

What is interesting here is the different uses material objects are put to and the means by which these objects are acquired and "appreciated." In his letters, Twain invents his alter ego, Brown, who is an avid collector of curios. Throughout their trip, Brown constantly attempts to collect what he calls "specimens": "As usual, Brown loaded his unhappy horse with fifteen or twenty pounds of 'specimens', to be cursed and worried over for a time, and then discarded for new toys of a similar nature. He is like most people who visit these islands; they are always collecting specimens, with a wild enthusiasm, but they never get home with any of them" (213–214). To Brown, the act of collecting these "specimens"— bones, stones, lava blocks, and so on—is more important than retention and more important than the land in which he, like Cook, is a tourist. The interchangeability between one keepsake and another is suggestive of an indiscriminate consumption in which the tourist enthusiastically indulges. As Amy Kaplan points out, "The collection of bones, specimens, talismans, or souvenirs does not simply commemorate or refer to a known place or historical event; rather, collections manufacture their own reference as a way of making tourists at home by both representing and disavowing the colonial violence that links the history of conquest to the present journey."[4] So it may sound like a case of barbed irony against the natives when Twain says "this is not properly a monument, since it was erected by the natives themselves, and less to do honor to the circumnavigator than for the sake of convenience in roasting him," but actually the sarcasm is double-edged. Keeping a roasting oven as a monument to the person whose flesh was roasted there is no more absurd than Cook's sacrilegious act of taking down the railing of his own temple and using it as fuel and shipbuilding material. These objects and sites are regimes of signs prone to intentional and unintentional misreadings.

Whether accidental or strategic, misreadings relate to one of the central motifs in Twain's Pacific writings: mislaying. Years later, when Twain passed by Hawaii again on a tour that would become the basis for another travel book, *Following the Equator,* he recalled a story about a white American boy who had grown up on the islands. Before moving back to the States with his parents, the boy had spoken only Kanaka (native Hawaiian language). But soon he lost his "first" language and picked up English. The boy grew up to be a professional diver. One day, as he descended into a sunken boat, he felt something touching his shoulder. He turned around and found "a dead man swaying and bobbing about him and seemingly inspecting him inquiringly." He was so frightened that he lost consciousness. The days after he was taken ashore and lying in bed, he was delirious and "talked Kanaka incessantly and glibly; and Kanaka only." At this point of the story, Twain comments: "Many languages and things get mislaid in a person's head, and stay mislaid for lack of this remedy."[5]

In *Following the Equator,* this story of mislaid languages and things is followed by another, about a Bill Ragsdale, whom Twain has written about in his Hawaiian letters. Half-white and half-Kanaka, Ragsdale worked as an interpreter for the King's court and had a great talent for moving across languages, "turning every Kanaka speech into English and every English speech into Kanaka, with a readiness and felicity of language that are remarkable."[6] What impressed Twain the most was, in Kaplan's words, not Ragsdale's facilitation of smooth communication, but the way in which his fluency seemed to yield him subversive power to channel the flow of that communication. According to Twain's observation, Ragsdale would, without departing from the original remarks and with apparent unconsciousness, "drop in a little voluntary contribution occasionally in the way of a word or two that will make the gravest speech utterly ridiculous."[7] A translation that is slightly off-key changes the nature of a speech. Such a "mislaying" of language recalls the uneven exchange of material objects and cultural beliefs between the natives and the whites, a process in which the content, value, and use of things and beings are constantly misconstrued, continually negotiated, or as Nicholas Thomas calls it, "entangled": Cook killed the natives who tried to steal (and collect) nails from his boats and ships, but he destroyed the natives' sacred grounds just to get some firewood. What the whites thought to be native women's wanton behavior turned out to be a necessity during the period of initiation, or, in a twisted manner, the white men had been abused by the natives for their own purposes.[8]

In spite of his apparent enthusiasm over the new age of the Pacific, we can identify in Twain subterranean layers of reservations, concerns, contradictions, and reversals. The Pacific, a passage to world domination for the United States but a lost world for the Pacific islanders, is by no means a transparent, pure, neutral, or objective space. It is, rather, a space of contradictions. For the precontact local Pacific islanders, the ocean is what Henri Lefebvre has termed an absolute space because it is lived through a preliterate phantasmagoria of religion and culture, giving the lie to Sigmund Freud's concept of "oceanic feeling." To Freud, this is a feeling "as of something limitless, unbounded—as it were, 'oceanic'," or "of an indissoluble bond, of being one with the external world as a whole."[9]

Such lived reality of absolute space would give way to abstract space when capitalism and Western technology moved into the Pacific. The outcome would be, in the words of Lefebvre, "an authoritarian and brutal spatial practice," because abstract space is a "tool of domination" that "asphyxiates whatever is conceived within it."[10] The best indication that Twain was aware of such critical changes of spatial practice in the Pacific can be found in what may have been his most famous piece of writing about Hawaii—neither his Hawaiian letters nor his pieces in *Following the Equator*, but a single phrase he once used in a letter. In 1908, on the occasion of the completion of Twain's Stormfield residence and his seventy-third birthday, the Hawaii Promotion Committee sent a gift of a mantelpiece and wall decoration carved out of Hawaii koa wood to grace the new home of the writer whose career had been tied up with the historical destiny of the islands. In his reply letter, Twain calls Hawaii "the loveliest fleet of islands that lies anchored in any ocean," a phrase immediately picked up by the Promotion Committee as the best advertisement of the islands.

On the surface, the phrase appears to be a description of the timeless natural beauty of Hawaii, making Twain one of the many American writers who have produced a romanticized, clichéd portrayal of Hawaii as an idyllic paradise. But as Stephen H. Sumida suggests in his critique of Hawaiian pastoral literature, Twain's writings about the Pacific islands often simultaneously produce and parody literary prototypes.[11] This phrase, in particular, while reinforcing the pastoral view, can barely conceal Twain's unique brand of satirical vision of history, which has been revealed over and over again in his Hawaiian letters. The feeling of the absolute, oceanic, and timeless ("loveliest" and "any ocean") that the phrase seems to convey is couched, as Sumida reminds us, in the metaphor of ships ("fleet" and "anchored"). Such an expression recalls his own "a line of fast steamers," which he believes will compress the Pacific time-space and offer a speedier means of U.S. expansion.[12] More importantly, the metaphor is also a reminder of the many ships, real or fictional, historical or imaginary, that enter the Pacific and transform the space from the natural and absolute to the abstract and contradictory: Captain Cook's fleet, Commodore Perry's black ships, Twain's *Ajax,* Melville's *Pequod,* and so on.

The devastation caused by the arrivals of such ships is now material for standard history books: crumbling social structures, chiefs abusing their authority, men abandoning their families, houses lapsing into decay, gardens neglected, the people becoming visibly indolent or decrepit, and the cheerful buoyancy of spirits superseded by listless demoralization.[13] Although historians still argue over the imperialist nature of such an account of the so-called native cultural decay, few can dispute the fact of drastic depopulation in Hawaii: the population of native Hawaiians, which was estimated at 142,000 in 1823, was reduced to 39,000 in 1896, one year before Twain's planned revisit to the islands.

In 1895, twenty-nine years after his first trip to Hawaii, Twain had a chance to visit the islands again and see for himself whether or not the historical dramas had played out as he had once imagined, advocated, and worried about. But he was utterly disappointed, not by what he saw, but by his inability to see. On arriving in Hawaiian waters, he and his shipmates learned that cholera had broken out on the islands and that they were not allowed to land on shore. The only thing Twain could do was to look at the islands from the ship and recollect the past:

> In the night we anchored a mile from shore. Through my port I could see the twinkling lights of Honolulu and the dark bulk of the mountain-range that stretched away right and left. I could not make out the beautiful Nuuana valley, but I knew where it lay, and remembered how it used to look in the old times. We used to ride up it on horseback in those days—we young people—and branch off and gather bones in a sandy region where one of the first Kamehameha's battles was fought.[14]

Such a shipboard perspective, rather than a view from the shore, is also the one Twain adopts in his expression, "the loveliest fleet of islands that lies anchored in any ocean." Twain is fully aware of the distance to the historical reality that he wants to see—"a mile from shore"—as he was aware, in his earlier Hawaiian letters, of the difficulty of finding "plain unvarnished history" that "takes the romance" out of the tales, valleys, and bones. Metaphors are lovely because they conceal where meanings are anchored, or mislaid.

2

Henry Adams:
In Japan and the South Seas

One's imagination is the best map for travelers.

—Henry Adams

The devastation of colonialism in Hawaii that Mark Twain was not able
to see up close in 1895 was something Henry Adams had been able to
experience firsthand a few years earlier. If Twain's account of Hawaii in
Following the Equator (1897) is full of nostalgia only because he has no
more "on-shore" testimony to offer, the curious absence of present reality in Adams's transpacific writings may be symptomatic of problems
that his famous *Education* has failed to address.[1] Adams's travel letters
from Hawaii often draw a picture of what he calls a "Kanaka paradise,"
one of timeless beauty and touristic comfort. "We had," Adams writes in
a letter to John Hay, "a dream-like establishment at Honolulu, a home
that left us nothing to desire except to stay in it."[2] As a result, his descriptions of Hawaii are at best clichéd observations of the natural
beauty of the islands, mixed with constant withdrawals into his own
fantasy as a replacement for Hawaii's reality: "I conceived it as a forest-
clad cluster of volcanoes, with fringing beaches where natives were always swimming, and I imagined that when I should leave the beach I
should be led by steep paths through dense forests to green glades where
native girls said *Aloha* and threw garlands round your neck, and where
you would find straw huts of unparalleled cleanliness always on terraces
looking over a distant ocean a thousand feet below" (*Letters* III, 271).
Relying on his own imagination as the map for traveling, Adams fails,
with rare exceptions, to note any political and cultural turmoil eroding
the social foundation of the islands.

In his insightful reading of Adams's classic autobiography as an
apology of imperialism, John Carlos Rowe suggests that Adams's hatred

of colonial facts is complicit with the kind of invisibility or deniability on which the imperial power of the United States has traditionally relied. The complicity is revealed in the correlation between what Adams has left strategically unsaid in the book and what Adams's alter-ego, Secretary of State John Hay, has done in foreign policies. The chiasmic dance between Adams's text and Hay's action becomes in Rowe's hand an intellectually rewarding exercise. To me Rowe's critique is strongest when he, unlike what he does in his earlier work on Adams, does not yield to the temptation of conceiving Adams's silence or equivocation as merely a modernist "compositional method" and thus making him yet another modern aesthete of irony and ambiguity. Instead, in his new work Rowe argues that Adams's literary "imagination," as mobilized in the *Education,* is the "intellectual complement to the imaginative work of the new foreign policy represented by Hay."[3]

But there is something else Adams has left unsaid in the *Education,* and that is his transpacific experience. The omission of the transpacific is not, as Rowe might suggest, merely another instance of Adams's collusion in the imperialist discourse of deniability or invisibility; it has specific geopolitical ramifications. As David Palumbo-Liu reminds us, at the edge of the Pacific lies what Robert E. Park in the 1930s would call the "racial frontier," a frontier that challenges America's ability to extend the European race and culture beyond its own geographical perimeters. According to Palumbo-Liu, "the Pacific represented a formidable challenge to modern America in terms of both race and culture . . . Many Americans retreated from that challenge and held firmly to a particular narrative of nation that stopped at such frontiers."[4] Adams shows similar symptoms of unease with and retreat from the Pacific frontier. He calls Japan a "doll-land" and complains bitterly about its smells, food, and women; in the South Seas he is equally troubled by racial hybridity and what he considers to be cultural backwardness. But unlike Richard Drinnon, who, in his study of Adams's transpacific letters, has simply condemned him as an outright racist, I want to suggest that Adams's unease with the Pacific and his ultimate exclusion of the transpacific from his autobiography is something more symptomatic than merely a case of racism or xenophobia.[5]

Adams's Pacific writings exemplify the limits and pitfalls of America's transpacific vision or, rather, double vision. In this bifurcated schema, the Pacific is seen both literally and symbolically—literally as an area of territorial/economic expansion and symbolically as an instance of historical/typological fulfillment. On the one hand, Adams describes the Pacific as a place of both cultural backwardness and pastoral romance that is devoid of history, and on the other, he dismisses the historical "worth" of the Pacific. Such a double denial—of history and of historical worth—may have accounted for the exclusion of the transpacific experience from his autobiography. The absence of the transpacific enables Adams to avoid a direct confrontation with what he calls the twentieth-century multiplicity and provides a rhetorical coherence to his idea about the unity of history. In this sense, the exclusion of the transpacific may well be a major rhetorical success—or rather, failure—of Adams's *Education*.

In Doll-land

"He stayed away, after this, for a year; he visited the depths of Asia, spending himself on scenes of romantic interest, of superlative sanctity; but what was present to him everywhere was that for a man who had known what *he* had known the world was vulgar and vain. The state of mind in which he had lived for so many years shone out to him, in reflexion, as a light that coloured and refined, a light beside which the glow of the East was garish and cheap and thin. The terrible truth was that he had lost—with everything else—a distinction as well; the things he saw couldn't help being common when he had become common to look at them. He was simply now one of them himself—he was in the dust, without a peg for the sense of difference."[6]

This passage is Henry James's description of John Marcher in "The Beast in the Jungle." James indicated in his notebook that he had based this story on the life of a "Mr. W," not Henry Adams.[7] But since James knew all too well the tragedy in his close friend Adams's life and his subsequent travels to "the depths of Asia," I am tempted to think that James had Adams partly in mind when he wrote the story in 1902.[8] The resemblance between Adams and Marcher lies not only in the theme of bereavement and belated love, but also in the travel to the East and the traveler's belated realization that the "garish and cheap and thin" glow of the East cannot really do much to restore whatever they have lost. That was exactly how Adams felt about his visit to Japan.

In June 1886, six months after his wife Clover's suicide, Adams went to Japan with his artist friend John La Farge. Adams explained the choice of Japan as the location for restorative purposes: "With the confidence that another six months will set me right, I am going to pass four of them in Japan, in the hope that where everything is upside-down, I shall find myself in keeping with the rest" (*Letters* III, 9). But this personal reason was only part of the story; Adams also chose to go to Japan because late nineteenth-century America had developed a craze for that newly opened exotic land, a craze that cultural historians have characterized as a symptom of antimodernism.

In the words of T. J. Jackson Lears, cultural elites such as Adams and La Farge were deeply disturbed by the "modern ethic of industrial rationality that desanctified the outer world of nature and the inner world of self." Consequently, they "recoiled from this ethic and groped for alternatives in medieval, Oriental, and other 'primitive' cultures."[9] Adams's notion that "everything is upside-down" in Japan was not only a metaphor for his own state of being after Clover's suicide, but also a commonplace of educated opinion in late nineteenth-century America about Japan. Percival Lowell, who spent years in Japan, opens his *The Soul of the Far East* (1888) with a similar statement: "The boyish belief that on the other side of our globe all things are of necessity upside down is startlingly brought back to the man when he first sets foot at Yokohama."[10] Japan's alleged contrariety provided a mirror—Lowell used the word "stereoptical"—for overcivilized America, presenting possibilities of other kinds of selfhood that predate rationalized modern identity. A prominent feature of such premodern selfhood is "childishness" or "childlikeness," a quality Lowell and his fellow Yankees had identified among the Japanese.

Adams was no exception to this ethnographic viewpoint. A week after arriving in Japan, Adams wrote to John Hay: "Of startling or wonderful experience we have had none. The only moral of Japan is that the children's story-books were good history. This is a child's country" (*Letters* III, 17). And he continued in another letter,

> La Farge and I . . . were playing baby, and living in doll-land. Just now we are established in our doll-house with paper windows and matted floors, the whole front open towards ridiculously Japanese mountains; and as it is a rainy day we expect our child-owners to come and play with us; for we think ourselves rather clever dolls as dolls go. As to the temples, I will enclose you a photograph of one. You will see that it is evidently a toy, for everything is lacquer, gilding, or green, red and blue

paint. I am still in search of something serious in this country, but with little more hope of success. (18)

Since Japanese were all children, they lacked seriousness in treating any-thing, including religion and death. Adams complained that

> Positively everything in Japan laughs. The jinrickshaw men laugh while running at full speed five miles with a sun that visibly sizzles their drenched clothes. The women all laugh . . . The shop-keepers laugh to excess when you say that their goods are forgeries and worth-less. I believe the Mikado [the emperor] laughs when his ministers have a cabinet council. The gilt dragon-heads on the temples are in a broad grin. Everything laughs, until I expect to see even the severe bronze doors of the tombs, the finest serious work I know, open them-selves with the same eternal and meaningless laughter, as though death were the pleasantest jest of all. (15)

The perennial jest Adams ascribes to the Japanese attitude toward se-rious matters such as religion and death may have been a trick played on his mind by the painful memory of his wife's suicide. (Later, in the South Seas, for instance, he is equally disturbed by the natives' seeming lack of seriousness in their mourning for the dead.) Likewise, the notion of Japanese childishness is undoubtedly an ethnographic bias or miscon-ception, one that apparently contains a grain of racism. But such an easy dismissal misses a crucial point: The manifest racism, rather than a jus-tification of cultural hierarchies based on *racial* distinction alone, may have also been a product of a particular *historical* discourse with which Adams has had a very ambivalent relationship. By this historical dis-course, I mean the progressive or teleological view of human history that has arisen since the Enlightenment, a meta-narrative that conceptu-ally polarizes human societies into civilized and barbaric, advanced and primitive, mature and childlike.

Before the Age of Discovery, European ethnographies about foreign lands—for example, the Orient—seldom characterize the exotic Other as childish or childlike. Usually, ethnographers describe those people as speaking in alien tongues, prone to superstition, and at most practicing barbaric rituals, but they do not associate them specifically with childish-ness. To describe the people he had come across in Asia, the medieval traveler Marco Polo, for instance, repeatedly made statements such as "They speak a peculiar language, use paper money, and burn their dead."

The notion of cultural immaturity is a result of looking at the world from the perspective of Universal History, a staple of Enlightenment thinking.[11] Hence to describe Adams's characterization of Japanese childishness as racism may partly be a misnomer because that characterization has as much to do with historical reasoning as with racial politics.

Adams's idea of history is a very complicated issue, one that begs for no less than a separate volume to cover it. But his ambivalence toward history as teleology is well documented. On the one hand, Adams remains deeply skeptical of the possibility that history fits into a progressive narrative. He calls time sequences "the last refuge of helpless historians" (*EHA* 91); and the *Education,* with its structural fractures and episodic digressions, testifies to the failure of a coherent historical narrative. Thus, Rowe presents Adams as "the archetype for the modern man of interpretation . . . condemned to the unreliability of his language." Joseph Riddel argues that the *Education* transforms the genres of autobiography and history into activities of "interminable reading" rather than conclusive realizations of self and education. And Gregory Jay maintains that Adams exhibits "the self-conscious collapse of the Hegelian model for historicism, in which History is narrated as the progressive, dialectical movement of Spirit's self-realization."[12]

On the other hand, skepticism over historical sequence is not Adams's only posture. Adams is firmly committed to what he calls the "Dynamic Theory of History," in which unity rules over multiplicity: "History had no use for multiplicity; it needed unity; it could study only motion, direction, attraction, relation. Everything must be made to move together" (*EHA* 359). Such a theory, with its principle of unity, is nothing but a grand narrative. Adams's allegiance to the teleological view of history is made especially clear when he applies the dynamic theory to international relations. As Rowe has showed us, Adams helped design and advocated his friend John Hay's imperialist foreign policy around the turn of the century. The so-called Open Door policy seeks to make diplomatic relations a reflection of the imperial will to unity by establishing an equilibrium among the major European nations and aligning the non-European countries accordingly as subject nations.[13]

Such a law is also manifested in the temporal difference inserted into the boundaries of race. Like his vision for a stratified world system, Adams's characterization of Japanese as children, implying that "we" are adults, is synonymous with the arrangement of races according to a spectrum of time. "For Adams," Howard Horwitz writes, "history exhibits unity because its teleological patterns are manifest through race."[14] In other words, the issue of race is inseparable from or even becomes a corollary to the view of history. R. P. Blackmur insists that Adams converted what was called the race question around the turn of the century (including almost every domestic and international issue—immigration, labor, the "Yellow Peril," "White Supremacy," etc.) to a "more universal and more potent level, as a part of history past, passing, and to come."[15] Racial discourse and historiographical paradigm seem to have reinforced each other.

It is much less interesting or intellectually rewarding to dismiss Adams simply as a racist than to treat him seriously and read closely his strategies of rhetorical suppression and containment. His ethnography of Japanese childishness, for instance, would not have sat well with the discourse of belatedness that he has rehearsed masterfully in the *Education*. Throughout his life, Henry Adams seemed to have been gripped by an acute sense of belatedness. He lamented time and again that he was a survivor from the seventeenth and eighteenth centuries who had unfairly been forced to play the game of the twentieth. He was too late for the glorious age of revolution of his forefathers, and yet he was unable to catch up with the new modern epoch. Coming back from Britain in 1868 to a country ravaged by the Civil War and witnessing the influx of immigrants in the docks of New York City, Adams described his feelings this way:

> One could divine pretty nearly where the force lay, since the last ten years had given to the great mechanical energies—coal, iron, steam—a distinct superiority in power over the old industrial elements—agriculture, handwork and learning—but the result of this revolution on a survivor from the fifties resembles the action of the earthworm; he twisted about, in vain, to recover his starting-point; he could no longer see his own trail; he had become an estray; a flotsam or jetsam of wreckage; a belated reveller, or scholar-gipsy like Matthew Arnold's. His world was dead. Not a Polish Jew fresh from Warsaw or Cracow—not a furtive Yacoob or Ysaac still reeking of the Ghetto, snarling a weird Yiddish to the officers of the customs—but had a keener instinct, an intenser energy, and a freer hand than he—American of Americans, with Heaven knew how many Puritans and Patriots behind him, and an education that had cost a civil war. (*EHA* 229)

A "belated reveller," Adams added, is someone who "flounder[s] between worlds passed and worlds coming, which has a habit of crushing
men who stayed too long at the points of contact" (84).

Such a sense of belatedness, of being stuck in the passage of time,
should not, however, be understood simply as an actual description of
Adams's position in the world. Both Adams's biography and the history
of modern America show that people with his kind of family background and wealth, with "many Puritans and Patriots" behind them,
fared much better than a "furtive Yacoob or Ysaac" did; and that, contrary to Adams's claim, they had a freer hand than, and an upper hand
over, the immigrants in the game of life and death. As Adams describes
in the paragraph immediately preceding the one quoted above, the likes
of him are actually leaders of the age of multiplicity: "Society offered the
profile of a long, straggling caravan, stretching loosely towards the
prairies, its few score of leaders far in advance and its millions of immigrants, negroes and Indians far in the rear, somewhere in archaic time"
(228). His persistent sense of belatedness, then, does not originate in his
real position in the world; instead, it may very well be a discursive pronouncement, a rhetorical position that he painfully enjoys taking.

Ultimately, the success of *The Education of Henry Adams* relies on the
delivery of the message that his education has made him a failure, a latecomer in the modern world. The discourse of belatedness constitutes in
a sense the bedrock on which the rhetorical success of his book is to be
built. But in Japan (and later in the South Seas), Adams faces people
who appear to be "far in the rear" in the historical teleology that he paradoxically both embraces and renounces. In this case, he becomes
strangely modern and not belated. To acknowledge such an experience
in his autobiography would be to undermine his well-rehearsed pose of
a latecomer and undercut his successful discourse of failure.

Bored in Paradise

"Tahiti! does the word mean anything to you?" asked Adams in the first
of his diary-letters to Elizabeth Cameron from Tahiti in 1891. "To me it
has a perfume of its own, made up of utterly inconsequent associations;
essence of the South Seas mixed with imaginations of at least forty years
ago; Herman Melville and Captain Cook head and heels with the French
opera and Pierre Loti" (*Letters* III, 402). Only a month into his stay,

however, Adams felt "bored": "I am bored—oh great Taaroa, known in Samoa as Tangaloa, how I am bored! Never have I known what it was to be so bored before, even in the worst wilds of Beacon Street or at the dreariest dinner-tables of Belgravia. My mind has given way. I have horrors. No human being ever saw life more lovely than here, and I actually sit, hour after hour, doing nothing but look out at the sky and sea, because it is so exquisitely lovely and makes me so desperately homesick; and I cannot understand either why it is so beautiful or why it makes me so frantic to escape" (445).

Adams left for the South Seas in August 1890 with a feeling that civilization is a bore, full of vices, causing him nausea (246–247). Only a few months later, in the midst of what was often characterized in South Seas literature as an Edenic landscape, he felt "sinfully bored." Why "sinfully"? Adams explained, "for I have nothing to do" (387). The lack of useful or interesting occupation creates a sense of boredom, which is in turn deemed sinful—such a moral sitcom actually allows Adams to play out his role as a bored beachcomber. But before I describe Adams's beachcombing, a few words on the cultural history of boredom.

The earliest detailed treatments of the emotional incubus known today as "boredom" were recorded in the fourth century. The hermits of Lower Egypt detailed their encounters with the *daemon meridianus* ("noonday devil"), visitations that devastated them, sapped their energies in the pursuit of God, and reduced them to blank lassitude, indolence, and despair.[16] As an English word, however, boredom and its variations appeared as late as the eighteenth century, in the same era as the ideas of "leisure" and the pursuit of happiness.[17] At its modern debut, boredom implied a moral insufficiency. As Patricia Meyer Spacks puts it, "The world that did not know boredom as boredom would necessarily have been one whose inhabitants believed in, lived by, a notion of personal responsibility" (11). That is, if you are bored, then you are morally insufficient. This notion has survived mainly in the domain of religious faith, where the complaint of boredom would violate the ethical imperatives of faith and good works (33).

With the arrival of the Enlightenment and modernity, the notion that boredom inheres in the consciousness of its experiencer vanished. What originally describes a subject ("If you are bored, you are boring") has come to describe an object. Progress should banish boredom by making life objectively interesting: a right to pursue happiness (22). Hence, the little fantasies we have every day, wishing "If only the lecture would draw to a close, if the school day miraculously ended, if a magic carpet could transport us to the South Pacific . . ." (14).

In feeling bored Adams faces a moral dilemma. On the one hand, it is a "sin," if not by out-of-date moral principles, then at least by the ethics of industrialism, that a man should sit idly and have no occupation; that's why he wrote to John Hay, "I think with terror what it would seem at home" that he was sitting around all day in the South Seas doing absolutely nothing except feeling indifferent and bored. "A son of Adams," Martha Banta writes in her analysis of the work ethic of the Adams family, "must resist the temptation *not to do*."[18] Or as Adams himself put it, "nothing but work will do" (*Letters* I, 558). On the other hand, the sense of boredom induced by being idle and nonproductive may also be a deliberately acculturated mental state, because being idle and nonproductive is exactly his staged protest against industrialism. Such a protest is not only manifest in his willingness to be a man without occupation, but is also embedded in his status as a tourist who is often described as bored and not getting any education from his trip.

In the *Education*, Adams rehearses this tourist theme. Adams reflects on his trip to Europe after graduating from Harvard, a trip often taken by young upper-class Americans to "see the world" before their debuts in society: "Nothing had been further from his mind when he started in November, 1858, than to become a tourist, but a mere tourist, and nothing else, he had become in April, 1860 . . . His father had been in the right. The young man felt a little sore about it. Supposing his father asked him, on his return, what equivalent he had brought back for the time and money put into his experiment! The only possible answer would be: 'Sir, I am a tourist!' " (89). In the eyes of his father, a tourist is someone who seeks superfluous experience of entertainment and not the serious task of education; a real travel—rather than a mere tour— should be taken as a secularized pilgrimage.[19]

But Adams questions such a conventional attitude toward tourism, as he continues to contemplate: "The answer [to his father] was not what he had meant it to be, and he was not likely to better it by asking his father, in turn, what equivalent his brothers or cousins or friends at home had got out of the same time and money spent in Boston. All they had put into the law was certainly thrown away, but were they happier in science? In theory one might say, with some show of proof, that a pure, scientific education was alone correct; yet many of his friends who took it, found reason to complain that it was anything but a pure, scientific world in which they lived" (89). An idle and bored tourist, then, may not fare too badly as far as education is concerned, for not only has all modern education been doomed by the age in which it takes place, but even the questions a tourist raises may be as important as what any renowned historian may ask. Sitting at sunset on the steps of the Church of Santa Maria di Ara Coeli in Rome, where "two great experiments of western civilization had left there the chief monuments of their failure," and where supposedly Edward Gibbon had first gotten the inspiration for composing his historical masterpiece, Adams writes,

> The young man had no idea what he was doing. The thought of posing for a Gibbon never entered his mind. He was a tourist, even to the depths of sub-consciousness, and it was well for him that he should be nothing else, for even the greatest of men cannot sit with dignity, "in the close of evening, among the ruins of the Capitol," unless they have something quite original to say about it. Tacitus could do it; so could Michael Angelo; and so, at a pinch, could Gibbon, though in figure hardly heroic; but, in sum, none of them could say very much more than the tourist, who went on repeating to himself the eternal question:—Why! Why!! Why!!!—as his neighbor, the blind beggar, might do, sitting next him, on the church steps. (92)

Looking from this perspective, the tourist Adams is indeed a modern rebel or defector who refuses to accept what civilization means in any profound manner and declares it instead to be a "bore."

It is the same tourist who is now sitting in a Pacific islander's hut, looking through the palm trees toward the ocean, and wondering what he will do next, "when there is no possible object in doing anything" (*Letters* III, 366). He spends his daytime in such conundrums, and toward evening he takes a native canoe or dugout and paddles out to the edge of the reef to look at the sunset. At night, he often attends some of the native dances called *siva*, which amuses him in the beginning but soon wears him out. Yet, it is one thing that a tourist reflects on the futility of the achievements of the civilization to which he belongs and quite another that he expresses contempt for the other's culture and attributes his own mental torpor to the inherent boredom of that particular culture. This is why we need to look behind Adams's discourse on boredom and see how it plays out differently in Rome and in the South Seas.

"What I don't know about Samoa is hardly worth the bite of a mosquito," Adams wrote to Hay. "I have been amused and have been bored. The amusement has been great; the boredom has not been small . . . They are, as far as I can see, the least imaginative people I ever met. They have almost no arts or literature or legends. Their songs are mere catches; unmeaning lines repeated over and over. Even their superstitions are practical" (*Letters* III, 362–363). In light of my earlier discussion of how the concept of boredom shifts its focus on the subjective moral weakness to a blame on the objective lack of interestingness, we may say that while in Rome the tourist Adams's refusal to acknowledge anything profoundly interesting in the ruins embodies a profound internal critique of Western civilization, here in the South Seas his boredom, which is supposedly caused by the inherent lack of interestingness of the native culture, is more or less an ignorant mockery of the Other. Boredom is, after all, what Elizabeth S. Goldstein has called "an experience without qualities," an experience "with the deficits of the self masquerading as the poverty of the world."[20]

Tahitian History

The "real worth" of anything, including a mosquito bite, is elusive when values are no longer intrinsic but dependent on shifting standards negotiated across cultures. This issue emerged constantly in the encounter between the Westerners and the Pacific islanders in the colonial period. Literature produced by Western explorers is filled with descriptions of how readily (and stupidly) the natives would accept "trinkets" in exchange for "precious" native objects. What is implied in these incredulous descriptions of an apparently uneven exchange is the notion that the Westerners alone are the true deciphers of value. But as Nicholas Thomas has argued, the early contact situation was actually one in which values and meanings of objects are up for grabs, or, at best, *entangled* between cultural systems.[21] Oral narratives, as Vanessa Smith points out, are especially such entangled objects in a contact zone where the seeming superiority of writing as a Western technology versus the apparent inferiority of orality as a native tool is intensely negotiated rather than taken for granted.[22]

Adams's volume of Tahitian history, which he had privately printed in 1893 under the title *Memoirs of Marau Taaroa, Last Queen of Tahiti* and then again in 1901 under the title *Memoirs of Arii Taimai E Marama of Eimeo, Teriirere of Tooarai, Teriinui of Tahiti, Tauraatua I Amo,* is one such entangled object that stands at the liminal crossroads of orality and literacy.[23] Adams describes the making of the book as an ethnographic process in which he acts as the anthropologist with a notepad in hand, the Tahitian queen mother as the native informant, and her children the interpreters/informants:

> The longer I stay here, the less I am bored. Being now thoroughly adopted into the Teva family, I find myself provided with occupation, for I have at last got them into a condition of wild interest in history. My interest appears to have captured the old lady, who astonished her children by telling me things she would never tell them; and as they had to act as interpreters, they caught the disease one by one, till at length they have all got out their pens and paper, and are hard at work, making out the family genealogy for a thousand years back, and tracing their collateral connections in every direction. (*Letters* III, 478)

Unlike Adams's multivolume *History of the United States,* which is a solely literate event, the text of Tahitian history is a result of an encounter between oral narrative and print culture. As such, it embodies many traces of that encounter, raises the stakes for the two sides involved in the joint venture, and throws into contrast their different beliefs, biases, and motives.

In the course of his ethnographic data-gathering, Adams keenly noticed the "mistakes" of oral narratives: "The old lady's memory is prodigious, but even she often makes mistakes. Marau tells me a story; Moetie (Mrs Atwater) tells me a different one; the old lady laughs at both, and tells it in a way totally unlike either" (*Letters* III, 478). To call variations of stories "mistakes" is a literate assumption, a belief that there can be only one truthful and repeatable account of an event. An anecdote told by Roman Jakobson may be relevant here:

> While Roman Jakobson was writing his reflections on Ferdinand de Saussure, near the end of his life, his thoughts turned to a Russian peasant he had met sixty years earlier. The man was a storyteller, practiced in the art of reshaping traditional tales in a personal, original way. He was utterly "incapable of telling tales in a monologic fashion," and

he explained himself to Jakobson this way: "Is it possible to tell stories for no reason at all? No, I come to the inn, we chat, and someone says, 'God does not exist!' So I retort, 'You're lying, you dog, how can it be that there is no god?' And I tell him a story about that. Now another adds, 'It's true, God does exist.' And so I tell him: 'Now you're the one who's lying. Where did you see God?' And I tell them another story, against the existence of God. I'm telling stories only for the sake of contradiction."[24]

Commenting on this anecdote, Dennis Tedlock and Bruce Mannheim write, "The idea that folktales could be told monologically, in repeated form from telling to telling, is a fantasy as far as Jakobson is concerned, a projection of otherness that betrays its origins in a world of written literature and individualist social philosophy." In her study of Pacific encounters, Vanessa Smith also suggests that "Duplication is the mode of validation of a culture of print . . . Research within oral societies indicates that the concept of exact replication is a literate imposition on oral notions of retelling." Smith documents cases in which the written narratives of some returning beachcombers were invalidated simply because their authors were unable to retell their stories without variations. Beachcomber texts, Smith argues, "with their less confident relationship to textual authority, retained elements of exchange associated with spoken language."[25]

Adams was no beachcomber; his approach to the project of writing Tahitian history is just that, *writing,* even though he occasionally did try to create an effect of oral narrative. The first edition of the Tahitian history, for instance, begins with materials sifted from European accounts, "dense quotation from the voyage literature act[ing] as a framing device for the narrated history of the Teva clan."[26] Treated in this way, the Tahitian history is both stylistically and epistemologically similar to Adams's *History of the United States,* using a great deal of direct quotation out of his primary sources, relying on statistics where he can, and deemphasizing the contribution of the interpretive scholar. Even though with the second edition there appear to be some stylistic modifications— "the historical treatise gives way to a blend of memoir, romantic adventure, and character study, while history-as-laboratory-experiment gives way to the less firmly masculine venture of storytelling, and the effort to efface the recorder goes to the extreme of surrender to the alien voice"— Adams consistently understands history from the point of view of literacy and never really sees any value in oral telling as history.[27] (For instance, at the 1883 meeting of the American Historical Association, Adams was quite irritated by the presence of a woman historian, Lucy Salmon, who, according to Adams, had only "female story-telling" to offer.)[28] At best, Adams treated the often self-contradicting stories told by the natives as raw material with which he was to work out a "real" historical text. Oral history, in other words, is merely history that has not been written down and is not essentially different from written history.

Such an assumption is reminiscent of Walter J. Ong's classic diagnosis of the ideological consequences of the literacy bias: "With their attention directed to texts, scholars often went on to assume, often without reflection, that oral verbalization was essentially the same as the written verbalization they normally dealt with, and that oral art forms were to all intents and purposes simply texts, except for the fact that they were not written down. The impression grew that, apart from the oration (governed by written rhetorical rules), oral art forms were essentially unskillful and not worth serious study."[29]

Adams's insensitivity to the issue of orality versus literacy stands in stark contrast to the attitude of another transpacific traveler, Robert Louis Stevenson. In his work, Stevenson demonstrates remarkable understanding of how the history of the Pacific encounter was also a history of the conflict and negotiation between oral culture and writing technology. Addressing the difficulties he was having with committing native oral narratives to paper, Adams tried to compare himself to Stevenson, whom he had met on a desolate island of the South Seas:

> I have stopped writing the memoirs because I found that, without the genealogy to hang it on, the narrative was always wrong or unintelligible; but every day a crop of new stories, legends or song, turn up, until a year's work would hardly be enough to put in shape. If Alexander Dumas had ever struck this *trouvaille* he would have made a wonderfully amusing book of it. Stevenson could have done it, too, but he never got in with the old lady, and only touched the outside rim of Tahitian history. His legend of *Rahero* is extremely well done, and has only the fault of being done with more care than the importance of the legend deserves. In reading it, one is constantly worried by wondering that he would have worked so hard on so slight a subject. Rahero was a very subordinate figure in history, and connects with nothing. The legends and poetry of the island can be made interesting only by stringing

them on a narrative, and Stevenson could have done it better than any one else, for he has a light hand, when he likes, and can write verse as well as prose. My hand is too heavy for such work, and here I am anyway only a passing traveller trying to find a moment of amusement to vary the wild monotony of island life. (*Letters* III, 478)

Stevenson's *Rahero,* mentioned in Adams's letter, is subtitled "A Legend of Tahiti." It is a story of the near extinction and rebirth of a clan. It centers on a rather obscure character, Rahero, who fortunately survived the massacre, kidnapped a woman from the enemy clan, and tried to restart a clan.[30] Adams might be right that Rahero is a minor figure in Tahitian history and that devoting a long, 600-line ballad to him may not have been worthwhile. But Stevenson saw it quite differently. As he wrote in a letter, "*Rahero* is for its length, I think, a perfect folk tale; savage and yet fine, full of a tail foremost morality, ancient as the granite rocks; if the historian not to say the politician could get that yarn into his head, he would have learned some of his A.B.C. But the average man at home cannot understand antiquity; he is sunk over the ears in Roman civilisation; and a tale like that of *Rahero* falls on his ears inarticulate."[31] It is interesting that Stevenson used the word "ears" because the sound of the Pacific languages has been one of the most sensitive issues for him in almost all of his Pacific writings. In *The Beach of Falesa,* Stevenson tries to capture the Pacific *linguistically*: the word "Beach" in the title refers not merely to a place but also to the language of Falesa, the Beach-la-mar that Stevenson prophesied would become "the tongue of the Pacific."[32] Stevenson called the book "the first realistic South Sea Story"—realistic because the bastard idiom that he used to narrate the tale, "a strange conglomerate of literary expressions and English and American slang, the Beach de Mar [*sic*], or native English," has brought everything alive and vivid.[33]

Most significant of all, however, is Stevenson's book on Samoa, *A Footnote to History,* which provides us the best contrast between Stevenson and Adams as historians of the Pacific.[34] Preparing for the second edition of his Tahitian history, Adams wrote to Queen Marau in December 1892:

To be amusing, the men, and especially women, must be real Tahitians with no European trimmings. Nowadays in Europe and America, we are getting to like our flavors pretty strong. We want the whole local

color. Tahitian society is frightfully proper, but in old days it was almost as improper as Europe, and very much more frank about it. The
memoirs must be risques to be amusing; so make Tati, I supplicate,
translate all the legends for me literally, so that I can select what suits
our time. (*Letters* IV, 135)

In contrast to Adams's desire for the history to be "amusing" and
"risques," Stevenson in *A Footnote to History* abandons his main vehicle
as a writer: narrative. As his literary agent Sydney Colvin puts it,

> he turned . . . from a sense of duty rather than from any literary inspira-
> tion, to the *Footnote to History*, a laboriously prepared and minutely
> conscientious account of recent events in Samoa . . . Later these inter-
> ests began to give place in his letters to those of the local politician, im-
> mersed in affairs which seemed to me exasperatingly petty and obscure,
> however grave the potential European complications which lay behind
> them. At any rate they were hard to follow from the other side of the
> globe; and it was a relief whenever his correspondence turned to mat-
> ters literary or domestic, or humours of his own mind and character.[35]

The alleged pettiness and obscurity of characters and events—Adams
mounted, as seen earlier, a similar accusation of *Rahero*—certainly give
the lie to the title of the book, "the footnote to history." It situates the
author at the edges rather than in the center of historical narrative. But
as Smith puts it, the self-deprecating title also "advertises a subversion
of conventional historical method which anticipates criticisms about the
historical unsuitability of Samoan material: its supplementarity to the
main text of global events."[36] This is a case of what Anthony Grafton, in
his elegant study of the footnote as a curious textual species, has described as "footnotes to history" giving way to "footnotes as history."[37]

In contrast to Adams's simultaneous attempt to romanticize the South
Sea islands (to make it more "amusing" and "risques") and Adams's tendency to dismiss the significance of Pacific history ("what I don't know
about Samoa is hardly worth the bite of a mosquito"), Stevenson tries to
"write large that small print to which the history of peripheral societies
is reduced in the grand narrative of empire."[38] As he elaborates in the
Preface, "An affair which might be deemed worthy of a note of a few
lines in any general history has been here expanded to the size of a
volume or large pamphlet."[39] But Stevenson was skeptical about whether
history written in such a manner would meet his readers' demands:

"Will anyone ever read it? I fancy not; people don't read history for reading but for *education* and display—and who desires *education* in the history of Samoa with no population, no past, no future, or the exploits of Mata'afa, Muliaiga and Consul Knappe?"[40] I emphasize the word "education" because it is Adams's paramount concern as a historian and autobiographer—what history can teach and which history is educational. Adams's ultimate dismissal of the value of his own volume on Tahitian history is symptomatic of his overall attitude toward the cultural Other—a theme I have tried to advance so far in this chapter: "I am anyway only a passing traveller trying to find a moment of amusement to vary the wild monotony of island life."

"History had no use for multiplicity," so claims Adams, "it needed unity; it could study only motion, direction, attraction, relation. Everything must be made to move together; one must seek new worlds to measure" (*EHA* 378). Oddly enough, such a historiographical vision for unity would preemptively defeat the subtitular claim of his *Education,* "A Study of Twentieth-Century Multiplicity." As we have seen in his experiences in Japan and the South Seas, Adams turned a blind eye to multiplicity and, as a result, excluded these experiences from his classic autobiography. If the rhetorical success of his book is predicated on the alleged failure of the kind of education he has received, we can see from the outside of the book a mind that has arrogantly turned away from the Pacific and refused to be educated by the history of the others. The missing chapter in Adams's *Education,* then, is the lesson of the transpacific.

3

Liang Qichao:
A Journey to the New Continent

In 1868, two years after Mark Twain wrote the twenty-five Hawaii letters that would win him instant fame in the American West—he would give immensely popular lectures all over the West Coast based on his Hawaiian experience—the United States signed a new treaty with the Ching government of China to consolidate the provisions under which cheap Chinese laborers would, as Twain had advocated, continue to be brought to Hawaii and the United States. This treaty would not escape the attention of prominent Chinese political reformist and historian Liang Qichao, who recorded these crucial provisions and their subsequent appeal in his transpacific travelogues. Liang made two trips altogether across the Pacific, once in 1899 and a second time in 1903. On the first trip he only reached Hawaii and had to return because of the outbreak of the Boxer rebellion in China, and on the second he spent about six months in North America. Both times Liang came into contact with Chinese immigrants and paid close attention to his compatriots' often difficult lives in foreign lands, a factor to be addressed in Chapter 9.

But before turning to the lives on the margin led by these transpacific travelers and to their particular modes of self-representation in history as exemplified by Angel Island poetry, we will first look at what Liang himself called his "journeys to the new continent," journeys that had brought paradigmatic changes to him as a Chinese historian as well as to modern Chinese historiography.

> There is a man in Asia
> whose name is Liang Rengong.

> Working hard for his country but to no avail,
> he had to trim his hair, wear foreign clothes, and leave for
>   Japan.
> Having lived in Japan over a year, studying and making friends,
> he became listless and impatient.
> It is a young man's ambition to travel broadly
> rather than stay in an idyllic place for long.
> Now he will go to the homeland of republican polity of the
>   world
> to inquire about politics, seek learning, and see the sights.
> So at the midnight of December 17, 1899 by the Western cal-
>   endar,
> he goes across the Pacific on a ship.

Thus begins Liang's "A Song of the Twentieth-Century Pacific," a long poem in which he describes his journey on the eve of the new century and articulates his new historical vision for the future of China and the world, for which the expansive ocean will set the stage.[1] Prior to the trip, Liang had lived in exile in Japan for over a year after a failed attempt to reform China's political system. While in Japan, as the poem tells us, he became an avid reader of Japanese translations of Western theories, from which he would adopt crucial terms, such as *revolution,* for his *new historiography.*

As a scholar and historian, Liang had originally been trained in the antiquarian school, which favors exacting research and meticulous documentation over abstract contemplation and moral speculation. This school, variously called Kaozheng (Verification), Han Learning, or Guwen Xuepai (Old Text School), dominated in late imperial China's philosophical and historical thinking. After the fall of the Ming dynasty to Manchu "barbarians" in 1644, Ching literati, who attributed the shameful defeat of native Chinese to the moral bankruptcy created by the Sung-Ming Neo-Confucianism, started to reject their predecessors' methodology. In contrast to Neo-Confucianist moral speculation and "empty discussion," Ching literati "stressed exact research, rigorous analysis, and the collection of impartial evidence drawn from ancient artifacts and historical documents and texts. Abstract ideas and emphasis on moral values gave way as the primary objects of discussion among Confucian scholars to concrete facts, documented institutions, and historical events."[2] As a disciple of this antiquarian school, Liang had in his early years believed that the authentic teachings of Confucius could be uncovered by means of rigorous textual scholarship. The reign of antiquarianism, however, came to an end by the middle of the nineteenth century when China's fate took a dramatic turn as a result of its clash with the West.

One significant intellectual consequence of this clash, in the words of Joseph R. Levenson, was "the contraction of China from a world to a nation in the world," a contraction that radically changed the Chinese historical consciousness.[3] This shrinkage of China's geographical self-awareness was accompanied by the enlargement of the personal self-consciousness of an ordinary Chinese, a process described by Liang as one of change from a villager (*xiangren*) to a citizen (*guoren*) and then to a cosmopolitan (*shijieren*). A small but significant symptom of this change is documented in one of the journal entries Liang had kept during his first Pacific trip and later published as *Hanman lu* (Travels to Hawaii): in the entry for December 19, 1899, as he departed from Yokohama for Hawaii, Liang decided to adopt the Western calendar thereafter in his writing.[4] This choice may seem insignificant, but it indicates, in the words of Leo Ou-fan Lee, "a paradigmatic change in time consciousness," which is in keeping with Liang's self-declared transformation from a provincial person to a cosmopolitan.[5] In the same entry, Liang goes on to defend his choice: "Someone may ask, 'For a Chinese to use the Western calendar to keep his diary, isn't this a sign that he doesn't love his country?'" Liang's answer is, of course, an emphatic No, and he reminds his imagined accuser of the Confucian notion of Great Unity (*datong*), which demands the standardization of time and measurement. Not only is the Western calendar the most widely used and most systematic in the contemporary world, but the places he will be visiting all use the Western calendar. Therefore, Liang argues, as a man of the world, he feels the imperative not to use the Chinese calendar.[6]

Liang's evocation of the Confucian notion was as much a strategic defense as an expression of his new historiographical vision that was to be fully articulated in his *Xin shixue* (New Historiography [1902]). In this revolutionary treatise, Liang absorbs the theory of evolution and relates it to the Confucian concept of "three ages." According to Liang, there are two kinds of phenomena in the world: those characterized by rotation, which should be the subject of natural sciences; and those characterized by evolution, which should be the subject of historical sciences. Old

Chinese historians, who for thousands of years have buried themselves in the sea of documents and have come up with nothing but annals of dynasties, have failed to capture the evolutionary essence of human history. They have unwittingly followed Mencius's idea of history as a cyclical succession of order (*zhi*) and chaos (*luan*), rather than Confucius's concept of the *world* moving from Chaos (*juluan*), to Prosperity (*shengping*), and ultimately to the Great Unity (*datong*). What Confucius and the subsequent Chinese literati meant by the "world" was more or less an ethnocentric synonym for "China," a "middle kingdom" of boundless scope. With the redefinition of the "world" (and of "China") by Liang's time, the term *Great Unity* will also have to be reconceptualized globally.[7]

Liang rehearses this reconceptualization in his writings about the Pacific, writings that will bring him together with the likes of Mark Twain, Herman Melville, Henry Adams, and other nineteenth- and twentieth-century transpacific travelers who saw in the ocean a historical destiny— only that they saw it from different shores. In "A Song of the Twentieth-Century Pacific," Liang draws a picture of the ocean as the stage for the unfolding of world history. As Xiaobing Tang has pointed out, "a central image in Liang's concept of history during this time was the 'great stage' of world history onto which China had been thrown . . . The world as a stage is fundamentally a metaphor that grows out of a temporalization of space, a dramatization in terms of a potential and progressive time."[8] In other words, the Pacific is by no means an ahistorical background; instead, the stage itself is historicized. Or, to reverse Walter Benjamin's formulation that "history becomes part of the setting," in the Pacific, the setting (the ocean) itself becomes history.[9]

Whereas Benjamin's conception of the collapse of history into setting contains a deep appreciation for decay in natural history ("In the process of decay, and in it alone, the events of history shrivel up and become absorbed in the setting"),[10] Liang's preoccupation with the Pacific reveals simultaneously a salutary acknowledgment of the new age and a saturnine vision of the future of China in this new age. "A Song of the Twentieth-Century Pacific" retraces the development of world history by applying the conceptual lens of Confucian three-age theory. "In the beginning there was chaos and then came prosperity." After the antediluvian ages came civilizations in the areas of the Ganges, Nile, Yangtze, and Yellow rivers, the Euphrates and Te. In the ensuing 4,000 years, however, the center of the world moved to the Mediterranean.

Then the dramatic shift occurred like a thunderbolt when Columbus discovered America, and the Mediterranean yielded its central position to the Atlantic. Magellan's and Cook's voyages into the Pacific finally brought the world together.

Here not only does Liang use Confucian theory to modify Christian typology (Mediterranean–Atlantic–Pacific), but he also revises the Chinese historical paradigm itself: he does not use the third term in Confucian three-age theory: *datong*. He uses merely *tong*, meaning together or unity. The reason is obvious, as Liang goes on to describe the reality in the Pacific region: the United States, adopting the Monroe Doctrine, is like a hidden dragon leaping out, full of energy and arrogance. Occupying Cuba in the west, the Philippines in the east, and the Hawaiian islands in the middle, the United States has made the Pacific its inner lake. In such an age of "survival of the fittest," the old and cumbersome empire in East Asia (i.e., China) is like a piece of fat meat, waiting to be devoured. Facing such reality, the scaffolding of traditional Chinese historiography is under tremendous pressure to either bend or break.[11]

In his prose travelogues, Liang meditates and laments the fate of China and its perilous position in the Pacific. Especially during his second transpacific voyage (1903), Liang follows closely newspaper reports on the speeches of President Theodore Roosevelt, who was at the time touring the West Coast and was touting his expansionist ambitions in the Pacific. In *Xindalu youji* (Notes from a journey to the new continent), a long travelogue published in 1904, Liang includes long excerpts of Roosevelt's speeches like this one:

> Before I came to the Pacific Slope I was an expansionist (applause), and after having been here I fail to understand how any man convinced of his country's greatness and glad that his country should challenge with proud confidence its mighty future, can be anything but an expansionist. (Applause.) In the century that is opening, the commerce and the command of the Pacific will be factors of incalculable moment in the world's history . . .
>
> When the 19th century opened the lonely keels of a few whale ships, a few merchantmen, had begun to furrow the vast expanse of the Pacific; but as a whole its islands and its shores were not materially changed from what they had been in the long past ages when the Phoenician galleys traded in the purple of Tyre, the ivory of Lybia, the treasures of Cyprus. The junks of the Orient still crept between China and Japan and

Farther India, and from the woody wilderness which shrouded the western shores of our own continent the red lords of the land looked forth upon a waste of waters only their own canoes traversed. That was but a century ago; and now, at the opening of the 20th century, the change is so vast that it is well-nigh impossible for us to estimate its importance. In the South Seas the great commonwealth of Australia has sprung into being. Japan, shaking off the lethargy of centuries, has taken her rank among civilized, modern powers. European nations have seated themselves along the eastern coast of Asia, while China by her misfortunes has given us an object-lesson in the utter folly of attempting to exist as a nation at all, if at the same time both rich and defenseless.[12]

Sounding not so dissimilar to Mark Twain's economic advocacy, Roosevelt's speeches are essentially what Bruce Cumings would dub the "Rimspeak." In his study of twentieth-century Pacific Rim political economy, Cumings captures a historical discourse that plays on the "tropes of dynamism and miracles" of the Asian and American Pacific region. Even though he considers the Rimspeak to be of recent origin (the mid-1970s when the United States needed to reevaluate the geopolitical and economic importance of East and Southeast Asia), Cumings recognizes that this discourse has a long genealogy: " 'Pacific Rim' was there from the beginning, soon after Commodore Perry's 'Black Ships' arrived in Tokugawa port."[13] Saturated in triumphalist economic imperialism and loud in its pronouncement, the Rimspeak drowns out the other kinds of discourses that speak to the dark side of transpacific imagination. These discourses are best represented by Liang's meditations on China's grim historical prospects:

After reading this speech by President Roosevelt in the newspaper, I felt frightened for days and failed to get the worry out of my mind. What was his point in talking about "role" and "purpose" when he said, "playing a great role on the world's stage" and "carrying out our great purpose"? I hope my countrymen will ponder this . . .

The general trend of world affairs is daily concentrating more and more on the Pacific, as those with even a little knowledge of world affairs will affirm. Why? Because this trend is converging on China, as those with a little knowledge of current affairs can also say. In that case, no country is in a better position to utilize the Pacific in order to hold sway over the world than China. But China is unable to become the master of the Pacific, and politely yields this position to others. How then can I bear speaking about the Pacific?[14]

From his earlier enthusiastic acknowledgment of the emergence of the Pacific as the new stage of world history, Liang has now turned to a saturnine vision of the geopolitical reality. Although his self-consciousness may have been expanded, as he claims, from that of a provincial villager to a cosmopolitan, his concerns have become increasingly nationalistic. As a strategic defense against Rooseveltian Rimspeak, Liang calls for "revolutions" in discourses that lie at the foundation of Chinese culture: poetry and historiography.

In Liang's discursive universe, *revolution (geming)* is a complicated term, bringing with it radically different cultural origins and connotations. The ambiguity of this term, as we will see, eventually provides fertile ground for Liang's reversal, albeit never complete, of his discursive positions on nationalism and historiography. The modern Chinese use of *revolution* was a result of a back-translation from Japanese that retained a semantic conflation of two incompatible meanings. The original Chinese usage of *geming* occurs in the classics such as *Yijing* (Book of Changes) and *Mencius,* where it means "following the people's will and depriving a ruler of the mandate of heaven to rule."[15] In other words, premodern Chinese "revolutions" involved the restoration of a preexisting order. Japanese, however, used the *kanji* term *kakumei* (i.e., *geming*) to translate the Western concept of revolution, which signifies drastic changes in societal structure. According to Jianhua Chen, it was in one crucial passage of *Hanman lu,* a passage in which he proclaimed a "poetic revolution," that Liang first used the term that had long existed in Chinese but now had been filtered through Japanese translation before picking up new meanings. "Although I am not a talented poet," writes Liang, "I will do my best to introduce European spiritual thought, so that it can serve as poetic materials for future poets. In short, the fate of Chinese poetry would be doomed if there were no *poetic revolution*. However, poetry can never die and a revolution is just around the corner."[16]

Disenchanted from the mandate of Heaven in traditional *geming* discourse, Liang's "poetic revolution" is not, however, a call for a complete break with Chinese poetic tradition. He explains his ideas along an unusual line of thinking that draws on an analogy between poetic creation and Pacific exploration:

> If you write poetry, you must be a Columbus or Magellan of the poetic realm. When the fertility of Europe's soils was exhausted and there was

a surplus of industrial production, the Europeans had to search for new land in America and on the shores of the Pacific Ocean. If you wish to be a Columbus or Magellan of the poetic realm, you must first develop three strengths. First, you need a new realm of ideas. Second, you need new language, and third, you must incorporate the first two into the forms of the ancients. Then and only then can you perfect the writing of poetry.[17]

Incorporating new ideas and language into old forms may sound like "putting new wine into an old bottle," but such a compromised revolution, which conflates two seemingly incompatible meanings, indicates the degree of difficulty in negotiating between Chinese cultural traditions and the new geopolitical reality in the Pacific.

But the negotiation was even more strenuous in the field of historiography, where Liang has also called for a revolution.[18] It is hard to ascertain the extent to which Liang's transpacific journeys have shaped his turn to nationalist historiography, but there is no mistake that in face of the expansionist rhetoric such as Roosevelt's Rimspeak, Liang feels the increasing need for a historiographical revolution that can serve China, which is no longer the "world" but merely a nation. One of the central themes in Liang's *Xin shixue* (new historiography; 1902) is that history should serve nationalism. Traditional Chinese historiography, which confines itself to erudition and compilation of facts, has not only failed to capture the evolutionary essence of historical development but has also fallen short of its proper aim to create and reinforce a national identity. Whereas earlier the Kaozheng School as the epitome of Chinese antiquarianism had replaced Song-Ming moral philosophy, which had been blamed for the fall of the native Ming dynasty to the Manchu Qing regime, now such antiquarian historiography has become utterly inadequate in the face of the new global geopolitics, which demands a new "spirit of history."

"What is the spirit of history?" Liang asked. "Answer: ideas. There are different social groups within a whole society; there are various stages within a long period. In the interaction among different groups and succession of one period to another, there are changes and causes. If the historian is able to detect the phenomena, understand causality, and, by looking into the past examples, foretell the trends of the future, his writing will then be of use to the world." History, Liang insists, is the only branch of knowledge that will unite and strengthen "the four hundred million compatriots in a world that observes the principle of natural selection." "Without starting a historiographical revolution," concludes Liang, "there can be no hope of redeeming our nation."[19]

But just as the word "revolution" in Chinese contains a semantic rupture between the old feudal idea of reform and the new modern concept of societal change, Liang's call for a historiographical revolution is not a complete departure from his own earlier training in antiquarianism. The fact that for someone like Liang, who is essentially a reformist rather than a revolutionary in politics, to call for revolutions in vast intellectual realms testifies to the profundity of the effects of his transpacific travels on his thinking. For instance, what has been described as the near extinction of the indigenous Hawaiian population since the arrival of Captain Cook—a sobering episode of Pacific history which concludes *Hanman lu*—has led Liang to resort to evolutionism and suggest that it is not the Europeans who have nearly wiped out the Hawaiians. Rather, he proposes, the Hawaiians extinguished themselves because they were unable to adapt to the new laws of world history and to transform their mode of historical thinking.[20]

But such a shock-wave effect, however profound for the moment, is not enough to flush out the residual elements that constitute the legacy of the premodern Chinese historiography Liang has inherited. Even though his *Xin shixue* was a treatise that revolutionized modern Chinese historiography by putting an end to antiquarianism, he would later come to recognize and reemphasize the value of antiquarianism as a method of historical studies. In his 1922 speech in Nanjing, Liang tried to revise the kind of objective scientism he had advocated some twenty years earlier: "There is no doubt that we should use induction to organize historical materials; but it is extremely doubtful that we could arrive at the knowledge of 'history proper' by means of induction. The effectiveness of the use of induction in historical studies is limited to the organization of materials and cannot extend any further in the field. To know history we have to rely mostly on intuition rather than induction or deduction—this is the key issue in the philosophy of history."[21] Such an emphasis on intuition recalls the doctrines of Chinese antiquarianism, which prefers concrete objects and multitudinous details to theoretical abstraction. Antiquarianism, then, has not disappeared without a trace in the Long March of History.

"The formal theory of difference," writes Henri Lefebvre, "opens of itself onto the unknown and the ill-understood: onto rhythms, onto circulations of energy, onto the life of the body (where repetitions and differences give rise to one another, harmonizing and disharmonizing in turn)." To Lefebvre, differential space, the fourth category of spatial production in his study, points towards what he calls "the truth of space."[22] If the Pacific, as Liang's writings demonstrate, is a space of differences, differences between Roosevelt's Rimspeak and Liang's saturnine vision, between Liang's two incompatible meanings of revolution, and between his new historiography and antiquarianism, then what is the truth of the transpacific space? Or perhaps we should back up a little and ask a methodological question instead: What is the best view of such a space? Bruce Cumings has provided us with one possible answer: parallax visions. Parallax, as Cumings suggests via the *Oxford English Dictionary*, is "apparent displacement, or difference in the apparent position, of an object, caused by actual change (or difference) of position of the point of observation."[23] China's clash with the West in the nineteenth century had already changed Liang's sense of position in the world (villager–citizen–cosmopolitan), and his transpacific journeys further radicalized his response to the new global reality.

My attempt in this chapter has been to delineate the fault lines in Liang's transpacific imagination, the fissures where the verbal energy flows back and forth between revolutionary vision and revisionary revolution. "Why," asks Lefebvre, "should spaces created by virtue of human understanding be any less varied, as works or products, than those produced by nature, than landscapes or living beings?"[24] This is a question we will continue to ask as we explore further along the other routes of transpacific imaginations.

PART TWO

Literature:
Moby-Dick in the Pacific

COL-LECT', *v.t.* [L. *colligo, collectum.*] 1. To bring together, as separate persons or things, into one body or place. 2. To gain by observation or information. 3. To gather from premises; to infer as a consequence. 4. To gather money or revenue from debtors; to demand and receive. 5. To gather, as crops; to reap, mow, or pick, and secure in proper repositories. 6. To draw together; to bring into united action. 7. To obtain from contribution.

COL-LEC'TION, *n.* 1. The act of gathering or assembling. 2. The body formed by gathering; an assemblage. 3. A contribution; a sum collected for a charitable purpose. 4. A gathering, as of matter in an abscess. 5. The act of deducing consequences; inference; [*little used.*] 6. A corollary; a consectary; a deduction from premises; consequence. 7. A book compiled from other books, by the putting together of parts.

COL-LECT'OR, *n.* 1. One who collects or gathers things which are scattered or separate. 2. A compiler; one who gathers and puts together parts of books, or scattered pieces, in one book. 3. In *botany,* one who gathers plants, without studying botany as a science. 4. An officer appointed and commissioned to collect and receive customs, duties, taxes, or toll.

—Noah Webster, *An American Dictionary of the English Language* (1846)

A supreme sense of serenity unfolds as the *Pequod* enters into the Pacific, into the "almost final waters" of the world:

> When gliding by the Bashee isles we emerged at last upon the great South Sea; were it not for other things, I could have greeted my dear Pacific with uncounted thanks, for now the long supplication of my youth was answered; that serene ocean rolled eastwards from me a thousand leagues of blue.[1]

Like Mark Twain in his famous description of Hawaii, which seems to register the timeless beauty of the islands but actually couches the expression in the metaphor of ship to insinuate the hard reality of navy fleets and gun battles, Melville also turns quickly from a moment of ecstasy to a more sober description of geopoliticized cartography:

> This serene Pacific . . . rolls the midmost waters of the world, the Indian ocean and Atlantic being but its arms. The same waves wash the moles of the new-built Californian towns, but yesterday planted by the recentest race of men, and lave the faded but still gorgeous skirts of Asiatic lands, older than Abraham; while all between float milky-ways of coral isles, and low-lying, endless, unknown Archipelagoes, and impenetrable Japans. Thus this mysterious, divine Pacific zones the world's whole bulk about; makes all coasts one bay to it; seems the tide-beating heart of earth. (*MD* 482–483)

In *Moby-Dick,* peacefulness portends the final and fatal confrontation with the White Whale. In historical reality, the Pacific sets the stage for the wars and battles to come among nations in the nineteenth and twentieth centuries. The "new-built Californian towns" and the "impenetrable Japans" are but two instances of the forthcoming historical drama. The Mexican War will allow the United States to claim California, and Commodore Perry's gunships will force open "that double-bolted land, Japan" (110).[2]

At the vanguard of these conquests, Melville says, is the whaling ship, "my Yale College and my Harvard" (112). "For many years the whaleship has been the pioneer in ferreting out the remotest and least known parts of the earth. She has explored seas and archipelagoes which had no chart, where no Cook or Vancouver had ever sailed." Therefore, "if American and European men-of-war now peacefully ride in once savage harbors, let them fire salutes to the honor and the glory of the whale-ship, which originally showed them the way, and first interpreted between them and the savages" (110). But if the College of the Whaling Ship teaches the success of conquest, the University of the Pacific instructs otherwise. "A moment's consideration will teach," Melville writes, "that however baby man may brag of his science and skill, and however much, in a flattering future, that science and skill may augment; yet for ever and for ever, to the crack of doom, the sea will insult and murder him, and pulverize the stateliest, stiffest frigate he can make" (273). The sinking of the *Pequod* is one such lesson the Pacific teaches.

In the long history of Melville scholarship, Ahab's mad pursuit of the White Whale and the subsequent sinking of the *Pequod* are usually interpreted symbolically, with persistent elisions of the geopolitical implications of Melville's simultaneous acknowledgment of the whaling ship as the vanguard of U.S. transpacific expansion and warning of the pending disasters brought on by such expansion.[3] By contrast, in my reading of *Moby-Dick* as the first canonical American literary text dealing with the transpacific, I look at whaling in the context of the U.S. pursuit of economic interests in the Pacific, which are inextricably tied to America's geopolitical ambitions and historical self-justifications. And unlike several recent scholars who are able to read Melville outside the symbolist framework but see him mostly as a willing or unwilling advocate of capitalist, imperial expansion, I want to complicate the picture, if not simply argue the opposite.[4] By looking at "collection" as a central motif that runs through *Moby-Dick* and by studying the subversive cultural poetics embedded in the antiquarian, anti-utilitarian mode of collecting, I argue that the book is a work of literature that unsettles the kind of transpacific interests expressed variously in nineteenth-century American economic and historical imaginations.

4

Collecting in the Pacific

The development of the U.S. economy after Independence was inseparable from the opening of the Oriental trade routes and the reaping of
the abundant natural products of the Pacific. On February 22, 1784,
shortly after the War of Independence, the *Empress of China,* a vessel
used as a privateer during the war and still fitted with guns, sailed for
China with a supercargo of ginseng, furs, raw cotton, and lead. The
transpacific trade was in large measure an attempt to rescue the young
republic's battered economy. After the war, the nation was suffocating
under a debt of over 50 million U.S dollars. To make matters worse,
markets accustomed to American raw products were limited or closed:
Great Britain refused to open its home ports on an equal basis to American shipping and closed its West Indies colonies to Yankee suppliers;
France also restricted American trade with its West Indies colonies; and
Spain continued its exclusionist mercantilist policies toward the United
States. Consequently, Americans had to turn to the Pacific in order to
overcome their nation's economic malaise, and they were in good luck.
The *Empress,* the first American ship to dock at a Far Eastern port, re-
turned in 1785 and made a 20 percent profit on invested capital. In the
following years, China trade expanded rapidly; by 1800, the number of
American ships that cleared Canton in one year had reached over one
hundred and in volume of trade Americans ranked second only to the
British.[1]

The boom in trading, however, was buttressed less by the native products of the American continent than by the natural products that merchants collected from the Pacific. Although the *Empress* was a success,

the Chinese soon discovered that the ginseng they bought from the Americans was not the same kind as the Korean herb that had been used in traditional Chinese medicine for centuries. Consequently, it became difficult for American traders to sell products brought from their native land. They had to look for alternatives and soon found that the Pacific abounded in natural products that would cater to the demand of East Asian markets as well as their home markets. Fortune seekers, therefore, moved into the Pacific to scavenge for furs, whales, bêches-de-mer, tortoiseshell, pearls, shark fins, bird nests, grain, fish, salt, coal, sandalwood, lumber, copra, copper, cowhide, tallow, arrowroot, vanilla, spices, guano, human heads, and human beings. These commodities gave currency to a nineteenth-century term adopted by Melville in *Moby-Dick*, "curios": the innkeeper told Ishmael that Queequeg had "a lot of 'balmed New Zealand heads (great curios, you know)" (19). Actually, the *Oxford English Dictionary* (2nd ed.) cites Melville's sentence as the earliest recorded use of the word.

"So if you want to know why Melville nailed us in *Moby-Dick*," writes Charles Olson in his idiosyncratic monograph *Call Me Ishmael*, "consider whaling. Consider whaling as FRONTIER and INDUSTRY. A product wanted, men got it: big business. The Pacific as sweatshop. Man, led, against the biggest creature nature uncorks. The whaleship as factory, the whaleboat the precision instrument."[2] By now we have become familiar with Olson's interpretation of whaling as a capitalist industry that extended the U.S. Western frontier beyond the continental limit. Regarding the whaling ship as a factory or a Pacific sweatshop may have identified correctly the commodification of whale products, whose value comes from human labor rather than the natural property of the objects. The decline of the whaling industry was a living testimony to its commodification: after petroleum was discovered in Pennsylvania in 1859, "kerosene, petroleum, and paraffin began rapidly to replace whale oil, sperm oil, and spermaceti wax as illuminating oil, lubricants, and raw materials for candles."[3] In other words, the analysis of whaling as a capitalist industry that is controlled by the logic of commodity may have sat well with canonical nineteenth-century theories of political economy. Olson, for instance, draws a parallel between Melville and Marx: "the year *Moby Dick* was being finished Marx was writing letters to the N.Y. *Tribune*."[4]

More recent readings of *Moby-Dick* also emphasize Melville's complicated relation to capitalism. Michael T. Gilmore identifies Melville's

America as a culture in transition from an agricultural society to a commercial and industrial one, and he perceives *Moby-Dick* as a "commercial epic." Paul Royster finds in the epic Melville's "deep commitment to the capitalist economy," although he also acknowledges that Melville eventually moved away from this position to "an outright condemnation" of capitalism in *Pierre*. And Wai-chee Dimock maintains that Melville's concern with authorial freedom is a demonstration of individualism as an ideological product of capitalist expansion.[5] Relying somewhat on a sophisticated, quasi-Marxist theory of economy, most of these readings have concluded that *Moby-Dick* is either an elaborate celebration or a literary reenactment of the capitalist mode of production.

But whaling is not completely under the control of the logic of production, and it is, as will be analyzed presently, even much less so in the eyes of a Melvillean collector. First, whaling as an industry is characterized by both fishing and manufacture. In classical political economy, human activities such as fishing, hunting, and fruit plucking, which may all be characterized as collecting rather than producing, are attributed to the primitive, precapitalist mode of economy.[6] They are not even part of what Marx has described as the process of "primitive accumulation" of capital.[7] Second, with the substitution of capitalist production for primitive collecting, a new mode of human relation both to each other and to material objects came into existence. As Jean Baudrillard points out in his critique of Marxism, in the nineteenth century with the coming of age of political economy, which regards production as the determinant instance, other types of organizing human relations that rely on magical, religious, and symbolic values rather than on the system of use and exchange values are consigned to the margins of the economy.[8]

In one of the most ambitious collections of the twentieth century, *The Arcades Project*, Walter Benjamin captures the essence of the activity that has been his lifetime passion: "The most decisive thing about collecting is that the object is released from all original functions in order to enter into the closest conceivable relation to itself. This is the diametric opposite of use and falls into the curious category of complementarity."[9] Here we need to differentiate two kinds of collecting: one is the capitalist practice of accumulating objects as commodities, and the other is what Benjamin describes here, a connoisseur's practice of assembling objects for the sake of what they are and not for what they are worth. The former is characterized by the stockpiling of objects, privileging those that have use or exchange values; the latter, according to Benjamin, withdraws things from the system of use and exchange, that is, the system of commodification. Benjamin believes that collecting integrates objects into a new, expressly devised system and encloses them within a magic circle. This new system is the collection itself, which displaces real time by turning it into dimensions of a self-enclosed world, into what Baudrillard calls a "pastime."[10] The magic circle is complete ownership or possession, which detaches the objects from their functional relations. Owning a book but not reading it, for instance, constitutes for a Benjaminian connoisseur the most intimate relationship that one can have to a book. In "Unpacking My Library: A Talk about Collecting," the bibliophile Benjamin writes:

> Of the customary modes of acquisition, the one most appropriate to a collector would be the borrowing of a book with its attendant non-returning. The book borrower of real stature whom we envisage here proves himself to be an inveterate collector of books not so much by the fervor with which he guards his borrowed treasures and by the deaf ear which he turns to all reminders from the everyday world of legality as by *his failure to read these books.* If my experience may serve as evidence, a man is more likely to return a borrowed book upon occasion than to read it. And *the nonreading of books,* you will object, should be characteristic of collectors? This is news to me, you may say. This is not news at all. Experts will hear me out when I say that it is the oldest thing in the world. Suffice to quote the answer which Anatole France gave to a philistine who admired his library and then finished with the standard question, "And you have read all these books, Monsieur France?" "Not one-tenth of them. I don't suppose you use your Sèvres china every day?"[11]

The nonreading of books prevents them from becoming what Melville would call empty ciphers, things meaningful only because of the contents that may be abstracted from them. Monsieur France's answer to the philistine's query rebukes the latter's utilitarian notion of books, reminding him that books, just like the china pieces stored inside almost every bourgeois household, have values other than use or exchange.

"Books," insists Melville in his 1850 review of James Fenimore Cooper's *The Red Rover,* "are a species of men," and therefore we need to relate to books in ways other than simply reading or using them. Actually, in this brief review, written when he just began to work on *Moby-Dick,* Melville says almost nothing about the book's content. Instead, he focuses on its cover and entitles his review "A Thought on Book-Binding." Melville laments the publisher's design of the book: "The sight of the far-famed Red Rover sailing under the sober hued muslin wherewith Mr. Putnam [i.e. the publisher] equips his lighter sort of craft begets in us a fastidious feeling touching the propriety of such a binding for such a book." He would prefer for the book "a flaming suit of flame-colored morrocco, as evanescently thin and gauze-like as possible, so that the binding might happily correspond with the sanguinary fugitive title of the book." To Melville, such attention to the "mere outside of the book" renders "any elaborate criticism of Cooper's Red Rover quite unnecessary and uncalled-for." He recalls that he once did *read* the book, but that was in his "uncritical days," a time when he, perhaps not unlike the philistine of Benjamin's anecdote, naively believed reading to be the only means by which one could enjoy a book.[12] A "critical" reader, then, is one who "would prefer not to" read. Here I intentionally adopt the famous parlance of Melville's scrivener in order to suggest that, like Bartleby, who refuses to serve the economy of exchange represented by Wall Street, both the Benjaminian collector and the Melvillean reader are also critics of the capitalist commodification of things. By their nonreading, they perform an act that is particularly destructive to capitalism.

As Karl Marx recognizes in *Capital,* production in a society must be a continuous process by means of constantly converting money into capital and putting capital into the sphere of circulation. To Marx, this constant conversion and circulation is the necessary condition under which capitalist production can take place.[13] The Benjaminian collector and Melvillean reader, however, take objects out of the societal system of circulation and thereby prevent, as long as the objects remain within their collection, any capitalistic conversion. In this way, the whole system of production is endangered. It may seem, however, that these objects are merely consumed commodities and that the practice of collection is therefore but a particular form of consumption, which in turn spurs rather than hinders production. But to understand collection in this way is to think only within the perimeters of political economy, which confines itself to the concept of utility. Georges Bataille, who introduces us to the important idea of general economy as the antinomy of restricted, utilitarian economy, draws a clear distinction between two kinds of consumption:

> Human activity is not entirely reducible to processes of production and conservation, and consumption must be divided into two distinct parts.

The first, reducible part is represented by the use of the minimum necessary for the conservation of life and the continuation of individuals' productive activity in a given society; it is therefore a question simply of the fundamental condition of productive activity. The second part is represented by so-called unproductive expenditures: luxury, mourning, war, cults, the construction of sumptuary monuments, games, spectacles, arts, perverse sexual activity (i.e., deflected from genital finality)— all these represent activities which, at least in primitive circumstances, have no end beyond themselves. Now it is necessary to reserve the use of the word *expenditure* for the designation of these unproductive forms, and not for the designation of all the modes of consumption that serve as a means to the end of production.[14]

The activity of the Benjaminian collector and the Melvillean reader, then, is better understood in the Bataillian sense of expenditure as opposed to capitalist consumption. And this is the reason that connoisseur collectors, as Benjamin is keenly aware, are fast disappearing in a capitalist society. Like the other types of nineteenth-century oddities with whom Benjamin is obsessed (e.g., the flâneur and the gambler), collectors are "figures in the middle—that is, figures residing within as well as without the marketplace, between the worlds of money and magic—figures on the threshold."[15] To these types, we may add a host of Melvillean characters: Ahab, Ishmael, Queequeg, and, above all, Melville himself.

As an endangered species living both within and without the economy of commodity, these Melvillean characters often possess a Bartleby-like obstinacy in pursuing their own objects and, as a result, jeopardize the very system that has simultaneously created and excluded them. Within the fictional world of *Moby-Dick* and the social reality Melville inhabited, those margins of economy are full of living struggles and undying voices. Like Melville's well-known marginalia, what occupy those marginal spaces—unintended as they are for "official" publication—often remain his deepest concerns. Whaling may well be a capitalist industry in the Pacific, but Ahab's pursuit of Moby Dick is more appropriately a process of collecting than of production. And such an antiquarian act, "unnatural" as it seems to the governing economic assumptions of the time, will create a rupture inside capitalism and bring the transpacific enterprise to ruin.

5

Ahab's Collectibles: The White Whale and the Yellow Tigers

Of what is Captain Ahab in Melville guilty? Of having chosen Moby Dick, the white whale, instead of obeying the law of the group of fishermen, according to which all whales are fit to hunt. In that lies Ahab's demonic element, his treason, his relationship with Leviathan—this choice of object which engages him in a whale-becoming himself.

—Gilles Deleuze and Claire Parnet, *Dialogues*

As a collector in the Pacific, Ahab is both a capitalist and a connoisseur, or rather a capitalist turned connoisseur. This critical transformation seems to lie outside the logic of capitalism and beyond the calculation of the Nantucket investors who hired him as the manager of their commercial enterprise. Ishmael repeatedly contemplates the irreconcilable duality of Ahab's collecting practice. Ahab was once "dismasted," lost a leg, and apparently suffered from "delirium at sea." "On account of such dark symptoms," Ahab's fitness for another whaling voyage should have been called into question. But

> the calculating people of that prudent isle were inclined to harbor the conceit, that for those very reasons he was all the better qualified and set on edge, for a pursuit so full of rage and wildness as the bloody hunt of whales. Gnawed within and scorched without, with the infixed, unrelenting fangs of some incurable idea; such an one, could he be found, would seem the very man to dart his iron and lift lance against the most appalling of all brutes. (*MD* 186)

They wanted to *capitalize* on Ahab's mad pursuit of Moby Dick, hoping that though he seemed ready to sacrifice all mortal interests to that one passion; nevertheless it may have been that he was by nature and long habitation far too wedded to a fiery whaleman's ways, altogether to abandon the collateral prosecution of the voyage. Or at least if this were otherwise, there were not wanting other motives much more influential with him. It would be refining too much, perhaps, even considering his monomania, to hint that his vindictiveness towards the White Whale might have been possibly extended itself in some degree to all sperm whales, and that the more monsters he slew by so much the more he multiplied the chances that each subsequently encountered whale would prove to be the hated one he hunted. (211)

The Nantucket speculators knew well Ahab's monomania in pursuing "that final and romantic object," but they did not foresee that Ahab's "prime but private purpose" would endanger the "collateral prosecution" of the *Pequod*'s voyage, what they deemed as "the natural, nominal purpose." Within an economy that values production and profit, growth and accumulation are "natural" processes. However, a connoisseur collector's private interest disregards what the investors have hoped at least to be "collateral" productivity, that is, fishing for other, commodifiable whales. (The refusal to *collate*, as I will discuss in Chapter 6, is the way in which the eccentric scrivener Bartleby resists serving a capitalist enterprise.)

The White Whale

In the following quarterdeck declaration of independence (independence from the Nantucket investors' commercial interests), Ahab reveals to his crew the "unnatural" purpose of the voyage:

> Aye, aye! and I'll chase him [i.e., Moby Dick] round Good Hope, and round the Horn, and round the Norway maelstrom, and round perdition's flames before I give him up. And this is what ye have shipped for, men! (163)

While Ahab manages to excite the harpooners and seamen by both the dramatic power of his Shakespearean language and the lure of his doubloon offered as reward, he fails to convince a real capitalist like Starbuck. The First Mate perceives correctly that the captain's private goal is in conflict with the ship's "real" business. Therefore, he makes his counter-declaration of independence—independence from the captain's private interest, and attempts to restore money as the measure of human activity:

> I am game for his crooked jaw, and for the jaws of Death too, Captain Ahab, if it fairly comes in the way of the business we follow; but I came here to hunt whales, not my commander's vengeance. How many barrels will thy vengeance yield thee even if thou gettest it, Captain Ahab? it will not fetch thee much in our Nantucket market. (163)

This verbal confrontation plays out the irreconcilable doubleness of Ahab's collecting practice: as captain of a capitalist industry, he has the duty to calculate and seek profit; but as an avenger of his personal loss, he pursues Moby Dick at the cost of the ship's potential profit. The way Ahab hunts for Moby Dick, characterized by Melville as "monomaniac," is essentially the way a collector goes after a desired item. Monomania, as Michael Paul Rogin tells us, began to be recognized as a disease early in the nineteenth century. Melville's father-in-law, Judge Lemuel Shaw, described monomania in the hallmark case of *Commonwealth v. Rogers* as a state in which "The mind broods over *one idea,* and cannot be reasoned out of it."[1] As someone who played a central role in developing a legal rubric for capitalist expansion at the time, Shaw identified monomaniacs like Ahab as people incapable of reasoning (an Enlightenment legacy) or cool-headed calculation (a capitalist quality), and thus disqualified Ahab, as Starbuck attempts to do, as an industrial manager. But Melville seemed to stand with Ahab on this issue and at odds, as he often did, with his authoritative father-in-law. "I stand for the heart. To the dogs with the head!" Melville announced in his famous letter to Hawthorne on June 1 (?), 1851. And he dismissed what he called "counting-room" calculations, which were essential to business and development.[2] In *Redburn,* Melville portrays Adam Smith's *Wealth of Nations,* a founding text of capitalism, as being dry like sawdust and useful only as a pillow.[3]

Fired by his desire for vengeance and attracted by the singularity of Moby Dick, Ahab wants to take the whale outside of monetary measurement, outside of the system of exchangeability and utility. If all the other whales are hunted as collectible items in the sense of capitalist accumulation of commodity, then Moby Dick, to use the parlance of Balzac's Sylvain Pons, is "the flower of [his] collection," whose value cannot be measured by money.[4] In this regard, Ahab is the opposite of another deranged nominal agent of capitalism: Kurtz in Joseph Conrad's *Heart of Darkness*.[5] As a capitalist collector of ivory in the jungles of Africa, Kurtz was ruined by the excessiveness of his desire to accumulate: "Evidently the appetite for more ivory had got the better of the . . . less material aspirations."[6] Kurtz became a threat to the company's business only because he had become physically ill and mentally deranged, not because he had based his collecting practice on a different economic principle. Thus, whereas Kurtz represents the horror of the capitalist, imperialist pursuit of profit regardless of humanity by pushing the goal to its limit in heart of Africa, Ahab embodies a critique of profitability by changing, literally and symbolically, the course of the regular, calculated pursuit before he runs the ship aground in the Pacific.

Ahab's antiquarian interest also manifests itself in his numismatic reading of the "doubloon." Many critics understand this Spanish gold coin to play a pivotal role in *Moby-Dick*. And they mostly read the doubloon with respect to its function as money, its power to signify and exchange.[7] Such interpretations may be germane to the utilitarian readings of the coin by the "brains" part of the *Pequod*'s crew (i.e., the white officers). Starbuck, for instance, sees in the coin "some faint earthly symbol," its capacity to speak and signify. Stubb, in spite of his curiosity about its "signs and wonders" and of his effort to "raise a meaning out of these queer curvicues," claims that he will not "look at it long ere spending it." And Flask understands the coin as being "worth sixteen dollars," which in turn are equivalent to "nine hundred and sixty" cigars he can buy and enjoy (432–433).

This set of readings by the white officers of the ship is the diametric opposite of those by the "muscles" part of the crew (i.e., the workers who are mostly colored and/or indigenous). Queequeg, who has tattoos all over his body, sees the signs on the coin not as signs that represent other things but as what they really are. He "compare[s] notes, looking at his thigh bone; thinks the sun is in the thigh, or in the calf, or in the bowels." He does "not know what to make of the doubloon," that is, as money; instead, he takes it "for an old button off some king's trowsers." Fedallah, the demonic fire-worshipper, only makes "a sign to the sign" and bows himself, taking the sun on the coin literally as is, rejecting the logic of mimetic exchange. And Pip, a village-idiot figure, does not even begin to *read* the coin as a text, but only *looks* at it like an imperceptible object: "I look, you look, he looks; we look, ye look, they look." In his "crazy-witty" muttering, Pip foretells the fate of the doubloon not as a monetary sign but as a would-be relic of the imminent shipwreck, an antique to be collected or "hoarded" by "the green miser," the Ocean:

> This is a pine tree. My father, in old Tolland county, cut down a pine tree once, and found a silver ring grown over in it; some darkey's wedding ring. How did it get there? And so they'll say in the resurrection, when they come to fish up this old mast, and find a doubloon lodged in it, with bedded oysters for the shaggy bark. Oh, the gold! the precious, precious gold!—the green miser 'll hoard ye soon!" (434–435)

A hoarded coin is either temporarily or permanently withdrawn from the system of circulation and exchange. In the case of the doubloon, as Pip prophesies, it will lose its status as sign and gain the function of souvenir, whose value lies neither in use nor in exchange, but in the mnemonic.

Ahab has undoubtedly a collector/hoarder's mind-set regarding the doubloon. His numismatic reading seeks a form of self-closure that Benjamin has conceived as characteristic of a connoisseur's collection. Ahab says:

> There's something ever egotistical in mountain-tops and towers, and all other grand and lofty things; look here,—three peaks as proud as Lucifer. The firm tower, that is Ahab; the volcano, that is Ahab; the courageous, the undaunted, the victorious fowl, that, too, is Ahab; all are Ahab; and this round gold is but the image of the rounder globe, which, like a magician's class, to each and every man in turn but mirrors back his own mysterious self. (431)

Against the utilitarian deciphering of Starbuck, Stubb, and Flask, who read the coin only with respect to its exchangeability and propensity to signify what is other than itself, Ahab tries to close the gap between the coin and itself by equating signs with himself. Although he initially offers the coin as the reward for the first to sight Moby Dick, that potential exchange is short-circuited because it is he who first spots the whale: "the doubloon is mine, Fate reserved the doubloon for me. *I* only; none of ye could have raised the White Whale first" (547).

Having claimed the coin for himself after the first sighting and thus successfully preventing its circulation, Ahab, however, restores it as a monetary sign by re-offering it as a reward: "Men, this gold is mine, for I earned it; but I shall let it abide here till the White Whale is dead; and then, whosoever of ye first raises him, upon the day he shall be killed, this gold is that man's" (553). But again, he quickly short-circuits the potential circulation by proposing another, perhaps more likely scenario: "If on that day I shall again raise him, then, ten times its sum shall be divided among all of ye." What he does not say is of course that in that case, he will again *collect* the doubloon and offer his crew monetary compensations in its stead. In this way, the doubloon is "set apart and sanctified to one awe-striking end": it will become a hoarded coin, a collected object, or a souvenir like Ahab's vial of sand:

> As Ahab, leaning over the taffrail, eyed the homeward-bound craft, he took from his pocket a small vial of sand, and then looking from the ship to the vial, seemed thereby bringing remote associations together, for that vial was filled with Nantucket soundings. (495)

Ahab's nostalgic gaze draws on the mnemonic and not the use or exchange value of the object. Nostalgic manifestations, says Svetlana Boym, are "side effects of the teleology of progress."[8] Susan Stewart believes that such manifestations are cultural symptoms of an exchange economy within which the search for authentic objects becomes critical.[9] Unlike commodities that symbolize the development of human productive force and the progress of teleological history, souvenirs and collectibles—as prime objects of nostalgia—turn the human gaze back to the past, not the future. Flotsam of time, wrapped in their solid singularities, they create a static moment, a whirlpool within the incessant forward flow. Ahab's doubloon and his vial of sand are both irreplaceable souvenirs and collectibles that authenticate rather than merely, like money, represent.

"Dollars damn me," wrote Melville to Hawthorne, "and the malicious Devil is forever grinning in upon me, holding the door ajar."[10] His father had fallen victim to the increasing abstraction of objects into empty, monetary figures in the market economy, failing to commit himself wholeheartedly to the world of Mammon. Allan Melvill's ultimate insanity and death had left the family, a widow and eight children, on the brink of complete destitution. Fleeing the world of empty ciphers, Melville found the idyllic valley of Typee in the South Seas, where there were "no destitute widows with their children starving on the cold charities of the world; no beggars; no debtors' prisons . . . or to sum up all in one word—no Money! That 'root of all evil.'"[11] Melville's picture of a noncommercial, moneyless paradise was in many ways a reconfirmation of Ahab's subversive numismatics and a counterimage of the Pacific expansion of American commerce as represented by the whaling ship. The only difference is that Melville deserted the ship whereas Ahab will run it aground.

Crouching Tigers and Hidden Dragons

A ship is a collection, of which Noah's Ark is the prototype. (For Melville, there is another Noah's Ark, that is, "Noah Webster's Ark" [*MD* 240], meaning the Webster Dictionary, which I will discuss later.) As commanded by God, Noah, the progenitor of collectors, based his guiding principle of collecting on reproductivity:

> You and your sons and your wife and your sons' wives . . . seven pairs of every kind of clean animal, a male and its mate, and two every kind of unclean animal, a male and its mate, and also seven of every kind of bird, male and female, to keep their various kinds alive throughout the earth. (Genesis 7:2–3)

Similarly, the stocking and staffing of the *Pequod* were based on the principle of productivity. In the midst of the "great activity" of getting the ship ready to sail, Ishmael does not forget to tell us that, in addition to "a multitude of things" that are "indispensable to the business of housekeeping" (e.g., beds, saucepans, knives and forks, shovels and tongs, napkins, and nutcrackers), there are things "upon which the success of the voyage most depends" that must be stocked *in pairs:* "Hence, the spare boats, spare spars, and spare lines and harpoons, and spare everythings, almost, but a spare Captain and duplicate ship" (95–96). To these should be added the "Knights and Squires" and other crewmembers of the ship, whose service is of course indispensable to the business of whaling. Yet, the staff comes with its spare, too; and this spare part is used to subvert rather than to serve the "natural, nominal purpose" of the voyage: it is Ahab's private collection, his hidden Asian-Pacific crew.

Variously described as "tiger-yellow" or "yellow boys," "dusky phantoms," "noiseless" and "outlandish strangers," these five stowaways constitute Ahab's secret workforce, whom he employs only at critical moments to chase Moby Dick and no other whales. Unlike the regular crew on the *Pequod,* whose relation to Ahab is one of worker versus manager, subordinate versus superior in a capitalist enterprise, these

five are virtually slaves owned by Ahab. Judging by their complexions, Ishmael thinks they are "aboriginal natives of the Manillas" (217). Starbuck
believes that they have been smuggled on board, which to him is a "sad
business." But the profit-conscious Starbuck also advises Stubb that as
long as it is "all for the best" in helping to get "hogsheads of sperm,"
then "never mind" the smuggling (219). Starbuck's intriguing oscilla-
tion from moral condemnation of slavery to disregard for morality in the
face of profit not only reveals the hypocrisy of the capitalist, but also
marks a difference between Starbuck's and Ahab's economic beliefs with
respect to slavery as a system of collection.

At the time Melville was writing, Western scavengers in the Pacific
were collecting not only natural material but also human resources.
The collection of human beings came in two ways: contracting and
blackbirding. The first was a system of recruiting workers under labor
contract. Mark Twain, as we saw earlier, documented the recruitment
system and its benefit to the U.S. economy in his letters from Hawaii.
The second was a system of involuntary servitude. *Blackbirding,* like
curio, is another term that came into being in the context of the Pacific
trade.[12] Analogous to the looting of Negro slaves on the coast of Africa,
blackbirding pertains to the transpacific slave traffic: Pacific region natives were forcibly seized, confined in chains aboard ship, and sold to
plantation, mine, and lumbering proprietors. A vessel used for blackbirding was called a "collector-ship," a designation that would fit the
San Dominick from Melville's famous slave-trade story "Benito Cereno."
The most infamous instance of blackbirding was the Peruvian slave
trade. From 1862 to 1863, almost three and a half thousand Polynesians
were removed from their islands by violence or deceit and shipped to
the minefields in Peru. Since these islands were usually quite small, with
populations numbering only hundreds, most lost more than a quarter of
their populations, many lost over half, and in one case the loss was
80 percent. Of the 3,500 shipped to Peru, only 257 were still alive in
1866.[13]

Ahab's secret crew are apparently the spoils of blackbirding, for they
are owned by Ahab as slaves, smuggled on board, stowed away in the af-
terhold, and made to work for their master. But unlike the *Pequod's* regular crew, who are waged ("laid") workers of a capitalist enterprise, these
five are in a way Ahab's private collectibles, who have been withdrawn
from their functional relations to the economy they would otherwise

have to serve. As laborers, then, they occupy a unique position in the *Pequod*'s microcosmic society.

As Marx shows us, a salaried worker in the capitalist economy disposes of his labor power to create commodities that are alienated from him and to produce surplus values that exacerbate his exploitation and oppression. He is related to the employer only in ways that his labor power is a commodity purchased by the employer, a commodity that is appraised with respect to its use and exchange values.[14] By contrast, in the master-slave relation, the master has complete ownership not only of the slave's labor and labor product, but also of the slave's labor power. It may be true that the master can dispose of the slave and thus alienate him like other commodities; but as Baudrillard points out, when one analyzes the stage of the master disposing of the slave's labor power, it is already an economy of production and market that one is analyzing and not the stage specific to slavery. "In the original relation," Baudrillard believes, "the slave, or rather the relation master-slave, is *unalienable* in the sense that neither the master nor the slave are alienated from each other, nor is the slave alienated from himself as is the free worker in the private disposition of his labor power."[15] There is, therefore, a relation of reciprocity between the master and the slave, or a structure of obligation in which the kind of exchange between autonomous subjects and the kind of mutual alienation as found in the employer-worker relation do not yet exist. Ahab's relation to his hidden crew, especially to Fedallah the Parsee, is one of such reciprocity. Although Ahab, as Ishmael observes, "seemed an independent lord [and] the Parsee but his slave," "still both seemed yoked together" and there existed "such a potent spell . . . secretly to join the twain." Portrayed as Ahab's "shadow," Fedallah has tremendous influence over his master: "even as Ahab's eyes so awed the crew's, the inscrutable Parsee's glance awed his; or somehow, at least, in some wild way, at times affected it" (537). As Ahab's private interest to pursue Moby Dick relies mostly on the work of his secret crew, he has built a stronger bond with his slaves than with his paid workers.

To claim such a reciprocal, obligatory relation for the master and slave is certainly not in any way to glorify slavery as a model human relationship better than that which exists in a capitalist enterprise. It is foremost my attempt to distinguish in Melville's work two kinds of human relationships that serve opposing economic interests. To look at slavery as a collection is to understand a human relation that is torn apart by capitalism. Collection in its original form does not serve the interest of an economy that is based on the principle of production and growth, on the notion that value is produced by human labor. In the same way, the unalienable master-slave relation, before being transformed into a mode germane to capitalism, serves instead the interests of an economy that are based on symbolic exchange, expense, destruction, play, and all the categories that are excluded by political economy. Such a human relation, as Marx knew well, has to be torn asunder before the capitalist interest in unlimited production and growth may be fully expressed and duly fulfilled. Replacing it is another model, one that exists between Ahab and his regular crew, an alienating employer-employee relation that has been depicted so vividly in a famous passage of *The Communist Manifesto:*

> The bourgeoisie . . . has put an end to all feudal, patriarchal, idyllic relations. It has pitilessly torn asunder the motley feudal ties that bound man to his "natural superiors," and has left remaining no other nexus between man and man than naked self-interest, than callous "cash payment." It has drowned the most heavenly ecstasies of religious fervor, of chivalrous enthusiasm, of philistine sentimentalism, in the icy water of egotistical calculation.[16]

Such an ice-cold human relation is represented particularly well in the story of Bartleby. When the employer thought he had gotten rid of his unproductiove employee, he prided himself in his "masterly management" of the affair: "The beauty of my procedure seemed to consist in its perfect quietness. There was no vulgar bullying, no bravado of any sort, no choleric hectoring, and striding to and fro across the apartment, jerking out vehement commands for Bartleby to bundle himself off with his beggarly traps."[17] The plight of Bartleby represents the ultimate alienation of human relations in a capitalist society.

Within the *Pequod*'s microcosm, however, two kinds of human relationships coexist, and their incompatibility leads to a disaster that Melville scholars have often believed to symbolize the imminent Civil War. There is on the one hand a manager-worker relation between Ahab and his regular crew, and on the other a master-slave relation between him and his secret crew. The nominal purpose of the ship's voyage is a capitalist pursuit of unlimited production and profit, and its fulfillment depends on the *productive* labor of the regular crew. But Ahab's private goal runs in the opposite direction, and its success relies on the *destructive* power of his secret crew. The five stowaways are said to belong to "a race notorious for a certain diabolism of subtilty, and by some honest white mariners supposed to be the paid spies and secret confidential agents on the water of the devil, their lord" (217). Especially Fedallah, who has predicted precisely the disastrous outcome of the hunt, serves as Ahab's pilot to the domain of darkness, his Angel of Death. Releasing the energy of these dark forces, the mad pursuit of Moby Dick represents the opposite of what Starbuck would call "duty and profit hand in hand" (219). And Ahab, instead of being a cool-headed industrial manager who carefully calculates productivity and profit, acts as a monomaniac tyrant who misuses labor power to a wasteful end. To borrow Baudrillard's words, Ahab's pursuit is not a useful discharge or a profitable investment, but rather "a gratuitous and festive energizing of the body's powers, a game with death, or the acting out of a desire."[18]

Paradoxically, the successful expression of these principles of Bataillean general economy is enabled only by the ultimate failure of the pursuit. The failing execution on the one hand relies on an original master-slave relation that can leave aside any consideration of profit and value, and on the other indicates the impossibility for such a human relation to continue its existence in a capitalist economy that considers only profit and value. In *Moby-Dick,* the doomed pursuit ends with the sinking of the *Pequod* and the collapse of the capitalist enterprise. In this sense, Ahab, with his collector's appreciation for the singularity of noncommodities and his precapitalist relationship to his slaves, becomes an anticapitalist in spite of his nominal role as representative of capitalism.

6

Ishmael, a Pacific Historian

As if predetermined by his biblical self-naming, Ishmael belongs in Ahab's subversive genealogy. This is seen not only in what critics have characterized as Ishmael's errant narrative art or antiauthoritarian personal character;[1] but more importantly, it is seen in the Ahabian relation he maintains to things and the antiquarian approach he takes to history. These two aspects are intertwined in Ishmael in the same way that capitalist expansion and its historiographical justification, both trademarks of the nineteenth century, were symbiotic in the westward movement into the Pacific. In his dual role of antiquarian collector and antiteleological historian, Ishmael, like Ahab, was a critic rather than a conspirator of nineteenth-century economic expansion into the Pacific and its accompanying historiographical rationalization.

A Careful Disorderliness

Even before his self-naming, the "Etymology" already evinces Ishmael's subversive penchant as a historian:

τ η,	*Hebrew.*
KηTOS,	*Greek.*
CETUS,	*Latin.*
WHÆL,	*Anglo-Saxon.*
HVAL,	*Danish.*
WAL,	*Dutch.*
HWAL,	*Swedish.*

HVALUR,	*Icelandic.*
WHALE,	*English.*
BALEINE,	*French.*
BALLENA,	*Spanish.*
PEKEE-NUEE-NUEE,	*Fegee.*
PEHEE-NUEE-NUEE,	*Erromengoan.* (xvi)

This list of words for whale in thirteen different languages appears to have been arranged according to an order that represents human history moving westward both in time and in space: from Hebrew, Greek, and Latin, through Anglo-Saxon, Danish, English, French, and Spanish, to "Fegee" (Fiji) and "Erromangoan" (New Hebrides Islands).[2] Analogous to what Ishmael later says about whaling: "There are some enterprises in which a careful disorderliness is the true method" (361), this list also contains a deliberate disruption of the seemingly smooth westward movement, the trajectory that characterizes the Western imperial universal history.

When John O'Sullivan coined the phrase "Manifest Destiny" in 1839, he merely gave a modern form to the old Puritan idea of *translatio studii* and its eighteenth-century secular variation, *translatio imperii*. In either its religious or secular version, the cachet of the typology lies in the notion that the center of the world has moved throughout history from the Mediterranean to the Atlantic and then to the Pacific, and that civilization has been carried forward by a single dominant power or people represented in historical succession by the Greeks and Romans, the Spanish and the British, and now the Americans. Bishop Berkeley's celebrated eighteenth-century verse, "Westward the course of empire takes its way," had become one of the most tiresome American clichés by the mid-nineteenth century. Or, as Melville acknowledges in *Redburn,* "Since the beginning of the world almost, the tide of emigration has been setting west, the needle would point that way."[3] Such typological thinking bolstered the morale of the Puritan pilgrims and became one of the founding principles of the new republic. In the second quarter of the nineteenth century, this idea of mission metamorphosed into O'Sullivan's justification for Jacksonian expansionism.[4] Thus, Manifest Destiny, bearing overtones of both Puritanism and the Enlightenment, became a nineteenth-century American motto of teleological history. And it was a historiography that marginalized another view that had flourished in previous centuries: antiquarianism.

Like the Chinese brand of antiquarianism described in Chapter 3, Euro-American antiquarianism, as a historical method, also relies more on erudition than abstraction, more on material evidence (such as coins, statues, buildings, stones, and relics) than literary sources. Since the turn of the nineteenth century, during which time Hegelian philosophical history had successfully replaced antiquarianism as the dominant paradigm of historiography in the West, the word "antiquarian" started to suggest the notion of a student of the past who does not quite belong to the profession of historical studies.[5] Antiquarians hold a view of history that is no longer valid to professional historians, who are mostly trained in Hegelian thinking. As Arnaldo Momigliano puts it, whereas historians write in a chronological order, antiquarians write in a systematic order; and whereas historians produce those facts that serve to illustrate or explain a certain situation, antiquarians collect all the items that are connected with a certain subject, whether or not they help to solve a problem.[6] In other words, an antiquarian is "interested in historical facts without being interested in history";[7] and "history" in this case, as in most cases since the nineteenth century, means philosophical history, which concerns itself mainly with identifying and interpreting teleological patterns in a succession of events. Hence to historians proper, antiquarians are merely connoisseurs who live in a static world with no sense of progress, because their tools of trade, namely, collection and classification, dispense with chronology and teleology.

The development of historiography in America before and after Independence reveals a similar kind of predominance of philosophical history over antiquarianism in the mainstream intellectual arena.[8] The early Puritan settlers were disseminators of typological thinking. The Founding Fathers of the republic were mostly "whig" historians whose investment in historical studies was motivated by their desire to substantiate their claims against England and to ensure their political survival. Herbert Butterfield characterizes the whig interpretation of history as a "tendency in many historians to write on the side of Protestants and Whigs, to praise revolutions provided they have been successful, to emphasize certain principles of progress in the past and to produce a story which is the ratification if not the glorification of the present."[9] The writings of nineteenth-century American historians show an even stronger tendency toward whigish generalization and romantic hyperbole. In a chapter entitled "Some Characteristics Peculiar to Historians in Democratic Centuries" in his famous book about America, Alexis de Tocqueville makes keen observations about his fellow-travelers in the new republic. Tocqueville draws a distinction between historians who, writing in European aristocratic ages, tend to be immersed in antiquarian researches and those in America who prefer to rely on general theories. In the former case, "the attention of historians is constantly drawn to individuals" who are believed to have determined every turn of events in history. Hence, the research is so intensely focused on the minutiae of these individuals' lives and thoughts that the connection of events, if there is any, escapes the historians. In the latter case, however, the historians "see a nation which has reached a certain point in its history, and they assert that it was bound to have followed the path that led it there." Therefore, they prefer to "talk about the nature of races, the physical character of the country, or the spirit of civilization," gigantic themes that have to be tackled with a teleology in sight.[10]

Back to the etymological list in *Moby-Dick,* the path Ishmael's Consumptive Usher has followed is no doubt antiquarianism, a model of historical thinking that is also adopted by Melville's other characters, such as Redburn, who calls his own experience in Liverpool a chapter of "antiquarian research."[11] After the nineteenth century, the outdated historical method found its place in philology, legal studies, and other disciplines in which the past is useful as the past. The Usher's etymological list retains such a past as a depository of historical details that are not subject to the law of generalization. The order of the list may appear to represent a version of universal, teleological history with its westward movement in time and space from the Mediterranean to the Pacific, but such coherence imagined by nineteenth-century historiography is rendered suspect by the last two items on the list: PEKEE-NUEE-NUEE and PEHEE-NUEE-NUEE. To Melville's contemporaries, these two Pacific colloquialisms must be strange words that have escaped the linguistic interconnections among the terms on the same list that share Indo-European roots.[12] The polysyllabic, onomatopoeic words rule out any possible coherence one may find in the close approximations among the Indo-European words. Items on the list as a whole, therefore, do not accumulate and generate meanings in the way that Puritan capitalism produces profit according to Weberian theory.[13] Nor can the etymologist "speak adequately" or "name the thing" correctly, as Emerson believes a poet can do. Melville marked the following passage of Emerson's essay "The Poet" in his copy of Emerson's book:

> The etymologist finds the deadest word to have been once a brilliant picture. Language is fossil poetry. As the limestone of the continent consists of infinite masses of the shells of animalcules, so language is made up of images, or tropes, which now, in their secondary use, have long ceased to remind us of their poetic origin. But the poet names the thing because he sees it, or comes one stop nearer to it than any other . . . The poet knows that he speaks adequately.

Here Melville wrote a critical comment on the margin of the page: "This is admirable, as many other thoughts of Mr. Emerson's are. His gross and astonishing errors & illusions spring from a self-conceit so intensely intellectual and calm that at first one hesitates to call it by its right name. Another species of Mr. Emerson's errors, or rather, blindness, proceeds from a defect in the region of the heart."[14] This last sentence contains Melville's implicit critique of Emersonian transcendental vision. If Emerson's etymologist is a poet who can see and name, Melville's Consumptive Usher is an anti-poet who doubts both this kind of vision and ability to name. The structural incoherence of the Usher's list suggests above all the failure of language to denominate the whale successfully, or the failure of imagination. Rather than embodying a universalist theme of historical progress, the list becomes merely a collection by a philologist who mimics and mocks such progress.

Similarly, the section of "Extracts," its encyclopedic format notwithstanding, suggests the absence of a referent that may transcend the multitudinousness of the citations, of a referential meaning that may be progressively approached and ultimately captured. These "higgledy-piggledy whale statements, however authentic," Ishmael warns, must not be taken for "veritable gospel cetology." And the Sub-Sub, however painstakingly he has put these items together, will fail to please the world and will go thankless (xvii). As Leo Bersani puts it, the encyclopedism of the extracts as well as of the whole book fails to be redemptive.[15] Such failure is actually attributable, as I will discuss in the next section, to the methodology Ishmael adopts as a historian of the whale.

An Ostentatious Smuggling Verbalist

Unlike Ahab's intensely tactile knowledge of Moby Dick, Ishmael's relation to the whale is at first glance literary. He calls his cetology "the draught of a draught," implying that in either natural science or poetry, human effort to study the whale remains an act of writing: "The sperm whale, scientific or poetic, lives not complete in any literature. Far above all other hunted whales, his is an unwritten life" (135).[16] While in the experiential world of the narrative the whale eludes capture, in the verbal reality of writing Ishmael has managed to assemble a huge collection to which he assigns an ultimate name: "Moby-Dick, or The Whale." In other words, his whale collection is unmistakably verbal.

Yet, it is verbal not in the sense that the collection consists of words that are representative of or exchangeable for something else. As Benjamin has pointed out, the essential character of an antiquarian collection is the nonexchangeability of its items. Collected objects are treated as what they are and not as what they stand for or are worth. In his cetological collection, words are to Ishmael what Moby Dick is to Ahab: Words cannot be exchanged for referential meanings, and Moby Dick may not be regarded as a commodity. As a historian of the whale, Ishmael differs from the other cetologists in that he sees whales *in* words rather than *through* them—words are his whales, and vice versa. He divides whales according to what he calls the "Bibliographical system": folio, octavo, and duodecimo (140–144). Consequently, his effort to capture them leads to a kind of historical discourse opposite of what he ridicules as "a transcendental and Platonic application" (446), an application that features the lifting of metaphysical meaning out of words, things, and events.

Considered a "Romantic art" in the nineteenth century, historical writing is supposed to capture the zeitgeist of an age by emptying out the materiality of the documents that come to their attention.[17] Historical study is an exercise in transcendental thinking. When a historian quotes a literary source, his interest lies in what he can abstract or deduct from the quote and not in the quote itself as a solid object or real event. As Emerson phrased it in the essay "History," "No anchor, no cable, no fences, avail to keep a fact a fact . . . Who cares what the fact was, when we have made a constellation of it to hang in heaven an immortal sign?" To Emerson, history is the record of one universal mind: "There is properly no history; only biography" of that mind.[18] To Ishmael, however, a fact is like a Fast-Fish that gets loose but remains recoverable as a fact; there is nothing transcendental about it. What is a Loose-Fish and what is a Fast-Fish? Ishmael explains: "A Loose-Fish is fair game for anybody who can soonest catch it [whereas] a Fast-Fish belongs to the party fast to it" (396). A quote, for instance, is a Loose-Fish that becomes a Fast-Fish to the one who quotes. And the thoughts of thinkers are Loose-Fish to "the ostentatious smuggling verbalists" (398). Considering "possession [as] the whole of the law" in the business of quoting and fishing alike, Ishmael believes a historian's task is to "copy verbatim."

To give us a (natural) historical picture of the whale, Ishmael relies on knowledge gained not through abstraction but by concrete means:

> In a ship I belonged to, a small cub Sperm Whale was once bodily hoisted to the deck for his poke or bag, to make sheaths for the barbs of the harpoons, and for the heads of the lances. Think you I let that chance go, without using my boat-hatchet and jack-knife, and breaking the seal and reading all the contents of that young cub? (449)

But gaining anatomical knowledge, though more in-depth than superficial generalization, is merely the first step in a historian's work. The next step is to present this knowledge to the reader, and this is the stage that marks the division between transcendental history and antiquarianism. Ishmael continues:

> The skeleton dimensions I shall now proceed to set down are *copied verbatim* from my right arm, where I had them tattooed; as in my wild wanderings at that period, there was no other secure way of preserving such valuable statistics. But as I was crowded for space, and wished the other parts of my body to remain a blank page for a poem I was then composing—at least, what untattooed parts might remain—I did not trouble myself with the odd inches; nor, indeed, should inches at all enter into a congenial admeasurement of the whale. (451; italics added)

To "copy verbatim" seems a quite Ishmaelian (and for that matter, Melvillean) trait. The immense physicality renders each occasion of inscription—though always called a copy, a "draught"—into an originary event. Even the inscribed person Ishmael finds a copy of himself in Queequeg, a tattooed "aboriginal." Their practices of inscribing/copying almost mirror each other, and the unwritten poem on Ishmael's body has instead been composed on Queequeg's:

Many spare hours he spent, in carving the lid [of his coffin] with all manner of grotesque figures and drawings; and it seemed that hereby he was striving, in his rude way, to copy parts of the twisted tattooing on his body. And this tattooing, had been the work of a departed prophet and seer of his island, who, by those hieroglyphic marks, had written out on his body a complete theory of the heavens and the earth, and a mystical treatise on the art of attaining truth. (480)

Such an act of writing, as Ahab exclaimed after "surveying poor Queequeg" one morning, is indeed a "devilish tantalization of the gods" (481). The writing both records a past and recreates a present; it celebrates each copy as an original and does not lament the loss of any origin; and it puts writing into a system of exchange temporarily, only to take it out of exchangeability permanently. This corporeal sense of writing ultimately makes each record of history an instant of nonabstractable opacity and each historian an antiquarian collector of irreplaceable records. The romantic art of historical writing is therefore displaced by a verbalist's ostentatious art of copying.

From Wall Street to the Pacific

As a copyist, Ishmael is no doubt a spiritual progenitor of another Melvillean scrivener, Bartleby. The departing point of Ishmael's Pacific journey, the "insular city of the Manhattoes," is also the place where Bartleby ended his life. *Moby-Dick* begins with Ishmael's contemplation of sailing as a way to avoid suicide ("my substitute for pistol and ball" [3]), but the temporary relief does not prevent his heir Bartleby from seeking death. All considered, we may say justifiably that "Bartleby" reimagines an alternative for the same scrivener, only this time he works (but refuses to produce) for another kind of capitalist enterprise—no longer whaling, but Wall Street finance and law. Hence, a reading of "Bartleby" may provide a more detailed genealogy of a typical Melvillean copyist.

"Bartleby, the Scrivener" is subtitled "A Story of Wall-Street." In addition to being a chilling description of human alienation, it is also a profound critique of the cultural logic represented by Wall Street: the economy of exchange. In the story, the first symptom of Bartleby's ill-fittingness within the industry he is supposed to work for is his refusal to proofread his own copies:

> It is, of course, an indispensable part of a scrivener's business to verify
> the accuracy of his copy, word by word. Where there are two or more
> scriveners in an office, they assist each other in this examination, one
> reading from the copy, the other holding the original.[19]

This process is actually called collation. To collate, as *Webster's* dictionary defines it, is "to lay together and compare, by examining the points in which two or more things of a similar kind agree or disagree." The *Oxford English Dictionary* defines it even more specifically as "to compare a copy of a legal document with the original, and duly verify its correctness." It is a process essentially of creating an exchange between a copy and its original; the validity of the copy relies wholly on the accuracy with which it represents the original, which holds the only key to authenticity and power. By the industrial law of exchange, Bartleby's refusal to proofread threatens to invalidate the copies, making his work completely unproductive. Looking from the typical Melvillean author's side, though, Bartleby may in fact enact what Ishmael has called to "copy verbatim": to celebrate each copy as an original and thus completely avoid the mechanism of exchange. But since there are other scriveners in the office who are willing to proofread his copies and thus make his labor useful again, Bartleby decides to take a more preemptive strike: "At all events, he would do no more copying . . . he had permanently given up copying" (32).

In the story, there are additional symptoms of Bartleby's aversion to exchange. He never initiates a dialogue ("he never spoke but to answer"), and he tries to keep verbal exchanges to a minimal level by either being nonresponsive or resorting to his idiosyncratically succinct expression: "I would prefer not to." He seems never to read anything, "not even a newspaper," and the only thing he does that comes close to reading is to stand looking at "the dead brick wall." He eats nothing but ginger-nuts, which are purchased for him by someone named "Ginger Nut"—the playful repetition on the names is an attempt to dodge the relation of exchange implied in the act of purchasing. Even when he does eat, engaging in an activity that inevitably suggests digestion and circulation, the ginger-nuts still seem to have no effect on him: "Ginger-nuts are so-called because they contain ginger as one of their peculiar constituents, and the final flavoring one. Now what was ginger? A hot, spicy thing. Was Bartleby hot and spicy? Not at all. Ginger, then, had no effect upon Bartleby" (23). And most remarkably, as the end of the story tells us, Bartleby used to work in the "Dead Letter Office," a place where carriers of human communication, after failing to reach their addressees to fulfill the task of exchange, were "assorted . . . for the flames" (45).

Such death of communication is foreshadowed by a chapter entitled "The Albatross" in *Moby-Dick*. The Coleridgean bird of omen is actually the name of a Nantucket whaler, the *Goney,* with which the *Pequod* came almost to "gam." (Ishmael had, in a previous chapter on the whiteness of Moby Dick, told us that "goney" was the name that sailors gave to the bird.) Gam, as Ishmael "learnedly" defines it in a manner of a dictionary compiler, is "a social meeting of two (or more) Whale-ships, generally on a cruising-ground; when, after exchanging hails, they exchange visits by boats' crews: the two captains remaining, for the time, on board of one ship, and the two chief mates on the other" (*MD* 240). But the gam did not actually take place between the *Pequod* and the *Goney.* As the *Goney* loomed like "a skeleton of a stranded walrus" on the horizon, the crew of the *Pequod* was not only saddened by its "spectral appearance" but also alarmed by an "ominous incident": when the captain of the *Goney* tried to answer Ahab's greeting, his trumpet fell into the sea and hence he "in vain strove to make himself heard without it." But the strong wind made his words inaudible. Ahab had to continue the one-way communication by loudly hailing: "Ahoy there! This is the *Pequod,* bound round the world! Tell them to address all future letters to the Pacific Ocean! and this time three years, if I am not home, tell them to address them to—" (237). The dash ends the sentence and the paragraph, indicating the absence of an address to which all the missives will be delivered. The Pacific, then, becomes a Dead Letter Office.

7

Queequeg, the Pacific Man

It cannot escape a careful reader that the *Pequod*, sailing east from New England, reversed the trajectories of the Puritan pilgrims' *Arbella*, Columbus's fleet, as well as Magellan's ships. It entered into the Pacific, "the tide-beating heart of earth" (483), in a direction opposite to the Westward movement that teleological historiography had delineated. But the sense of itinerary reversal lies elsewhere as well in the book, particularly in Queequeg's personal trajectory from the Pacific to New England: Queequeg goes in a direction opposite to a Yankee frontiersman in the Pacific. But the inversion will in turn be replicated by Ishmael as he returns from the shipwreck to tell the story: Ishmael survives by hanging onto Queequeg's carved coffin.

A Mockery of Exchange

The sharing of a deathbed takes us back to the beginning of the narrative when the two were literally bedfellows at the Spouter-Inn owned by a Peter *Coffin*. Traveling to New England from Polynesia, Queequeg mirrors in many ways a Yankee who goes to the Pacific. Like some Yankee of blueblooded origin, he is from a royal island family. Like a Yankee scavenger, he collects curios (human skulls) from the South Seas and peddles them in the New England market. And like any decent Yankee, he has a religion, attends Christian sermons, and even "reads" the Large Book (although his "reading," as I will show presently, is a remarkable way of dealing with a text). As Ishmael puts it, "though an old idolator at heart, he yet lived among these Christians, wore their clothes, and tried to talk their gibberish" (56). But Queequeg does all these Yankee things differently and, in so doing, becomes "Washington cannibalistically developed," Washington being the symbolic progenitor of and a popular name for the citizens of this Christian country.

Ishmael painstakingly describes the exchangeability of Queequeg with a Yankee but also repeatedly suggests that the exchange would have undermined the value system on which the Yankee's world is based, for Queequeg carries on Yankee ways only to mock them. To start, Queequeg's "outlandish" appearance may astonish a Yankee, but as Ishmael admits, "at Bombay, in the Apollo Green, live Yankees have often scared the natives" (31). To counter Ishmael's friendly ridicule of his ignorance about how to use a wheelbarrow (he carries it on his shoulders), Queequeg tells an anecdote about a captain of "a certain grand merchant ship" who attended a Pacific island wedding ceremony and did not know anything about the use of the punch bowl ("the Captain coolly proceeds to wash his hands in the punch bowl;—taking it I suppose for a huge finger-glass"). "Now," says Queequeg, "what you tink now?—Didn't our people laugh?" (59).

It is true that Queequeg is a head-peddler who tries to make a profit, and in this sense he may be equal to a Yankee scavenger. But his attitude toward money makes him a kind of collector more like Ahab and Ishmael than a capitalist. In the aforementioned scene of the doubloon, Queequeg fails to see the coin as money, taking it instead "for an old button off some king's trowsers" (434). When he does recognize money, he has a potlatch mentality regarding wealth, which is more congruous with Bataillean general economy rather than with the culture of commodity:

> After supper, and another social chat and smoke, [Ishmael writes,] we went to our room together. He made me a present of his embalmed head; took out his enormous tobacco wallet, and groping under the tobacco, drew out some thirty dollars in silver; then spreading them on the table, and mechanically dividing them into two equal portions, pushed one of them towards me, and said it was mine. I was going to remonstrate; but he silenced me by pouring them into my trowsers' pockets. I let them stay. (51)

Such an act of sharing may be interpreted as an example of Queequeg's personal generosity and his high regard for friendship, but I also want to stress the stark contrast between the warm human relationship described here and the one Marx has called a nexus of "cash payment." Buttressing the friendship is Queequeg's nonchalance toward money, as much as undergirding the alienating human relation in a capitalist society is the fetishization of money. Hence, like his "married" bedfellow Ishmael, Queequeg is quite out of place in a civilization that is founded on the principles of monetary exchange. Melville presents his seeming similarity to a Yankee perhaps only to mock the Yankee way of life. Interestingly, the Melville who came back from four years of the Pacific journey had the appearance of a "savage"; his brother had to ask him to shave his beard and cut his hair in order to look more like a "Christian" before he met his family.

Counting as Reading

Among Queequeg's subversive traits, however, his relationship to writing brings him closest to Ishmael and by implication to Melville. As aforesaid, his tattooed body is an emblem of writing as a devilish tantalizing art. Those hieroglyphic marks carved on him are mysteries that are not subject to any hermeneutic interpretation: "these mysteries were therefore destined in the end to moulder away with the living parchment whereon they were inscribed, and so be unsolved to the last" (481). What's at stake here is actually less about mysteries themselves than about a kind of writing whose physicality blocks any penetrating, reductive reading. As Elizabeth Renker has demonstrated, Melville's relation to writing was a material relation, an engagement with "pages as an obscuring, frustrating, resistant force against whose powers of blankness he battled as he wrote."[1] Similarly, the physicality or materiality of writing creates for Queequeg an antithesis to exchange economy.

Although Ishmael says specifically that Queequeg does not know how to read (36), there is one scene in which Queequeg performs an act that mocks the mode of reading analogous to the prevailing logic of cultural production in New England. As Ishmael observes:

> Pretty soon, going to the table, [Queequeg] took up a large book there, and placing it on his lap began counting the pages with deliberate regularity; at every fiftieth page—as I fancied—stopping a moment, looking vacantly around him, and giving utterance to a long-drawn gurgling whistle of astonishment. He then began again at the next fifty. (49)

"Counting," as much as "calculation," is a loaded word in the economic world Melville has depicted for us. As Patricia Cline Cohen shows in *A Calculating People,* the flowering of numeracy, as evidenced by the sudden authority and ubiquity of numbers and statistics, profoundly shaped the character of Jacksonian America.[2] Alexis de Tocqueville, visiting America in 1830, observed the same effect of the market economy on the mentality of the people. "Their minds," Tocqueville said, were "accustomed to definite calculations."[3] As someone sitting uneasily with the market, Melville criticizes "counting-room" calculations that characterize business, and he calls the Puritan capitalists of Nantucket "the calculating people of that prudent isle." In *Moby-Dick,* Ahab becomes an enemy to business with his resistance to calculating potential loss or profit. He mocks "the accountants [who] have computed their great counting-house the globe, by girdling it with guineas, one to every three parts of an inch" (163); and he uses calculating tools (e.g., his quadrant, compass, and chart) to a wasteful end. Queequeg's elementary way of counting pages (these are not just pages of an ordinary book but possibly leaves of the Bible) obviates scriptural exegesis that would have led to a revelation of transcendental meanings as the profit of reading. Moreover, it implies that a book is a collection of concrete materials potentially resistant to semiotic exchange. When reading is counting, words lose their exchange value as linguistic signs but they retain their materiality as objects. What is *Moby-Dick?* It is, as the other part of the title indicates, "a whale," one that consists of head, tail, nose, heart, sperm, oil, lung, and all the other body parts. It is a giant collection, in the same way as the book in reality was created by assembling speeches, pamphlets, reviews, and newspaper articles from Melville's contemporary world.[4] These direct and indirect quotations are collectibles amassed to create a magic encyclopedia, which is the whale.

Stutter Is the Plot

But the encyclopedia refuses to reveal any coherent meaning, and Queequeg's "large book" does not provide him any hermeneutic satisfaction. This is why *Moby-Dick* is, as Melville calls it, a "botch";[5] and Melville may only stutter, as does his handsome sailor Billy Budd, as does his savage Queequeg. In Queequeg's case, it is not really a pathological speech impediment, but in the linguistic, literary sense. He is not native to English and speaks the Christian tongue—Melville calls it "gibberish"—with stuttering brokenness. Responding to Ishmael's own nervous "stammering" when they first met in bed, Queequeg gave out these "guttural" words: "Who-e debel you? . . . you no speak-e, dam-me, I kill-e" (23). "Stutter is the plot," says Charles Olson in regard to Billy Budd, whom Olson calls the Latter-day Ishmael.[6] And Susan Howe insists, "*Moby-Dick* is a giant stutter in the manner of [Cotton Mather's] *Magnalia Christi Americana*."[7] Both Olson and Howe end their books with a remarkable insight into the future of nations and the stuttering actors caught in conflicts. "Continents have entered into contact," writes Howe, "creating a zone of catastrophic points . . . We have come on to the stage stammering."[8] And Olson concludes *Call Me Ishmael* with a section entitled "Pacific man," his epithet for characters real and fictional: Ahab, Ishmael, Melville, Columbus, Captain Pollard, Commodore Perry, and very possibly Olson himself.[9] But the actual Pacific man in *Moby-Dick*, who appears on the new historical stage stammering, is Queequeg.[10]

8

Melville's Pacific Becoming: Fancy, Fate, Finis

To leave, to escape, is to trace a line. The highest aim of literature, according to Lawrence, is "To leave, to leave, to escape . . . to cross the horizon, enter into another life . . . It is thus that Melville finds himself in the middle of the Pacific. He has really crossed the line of horizon." The line of flight is a deterritorialization.

—Gilles Deleuze and Claire Parnet, *Dialogues*

Melville, too, is a Pacific man. *Typee,* a semiautobiography based on his adventures in the South Seas, is an account of his Pacific becoming. Even if the reliability of his stories is often in doubt—an issue that has both plagued and benefited the book—we would have to agree with D. H. Lawrence that naïve realism pales against Melville's fantasy of becoming a Pacific man: "Melville at his best invariably wrote from a sort of dreamself, so that events which he relates as actual fact have indeed a far deeper reference to his own soul, his own inner life."[1] Unlike Lawrence, however, my interest in Melville's Pacific becoming lies not in diving deeper into his soul, but in exploring the passage to his soul—not the ideological contents of his narrative, but the material forms of his Pacific writing. An often lamented feature of Melville's work is his penchant for digression. In *Typee,* those "otherwise unwarranted digressions" lead to repeated "returns" to the main line of narrative.[2] But such returns are not symbolic homecomings, but re-turns, re-directions. Becoming, writes Elisabeth Grosz, opposes "the concepts of directionality, progress, development, accumulation, and lineage."[3] In *Moby-Dick,* such critique of directionality and other concepts by means of what Deleuze and Parnet have characterized as Melville's "line of flight" becomes quite striking, especially when considered against the backdrop of another cultural geometry—Emerson's circle.

In his 1839 essay "Circles," Emerson regards the round shape as the "highest emblem in the cipher of the world": "The eye is the first circle; the horizon which it forms is the second; and throughout nature this primary figure is repeated without end." To many, Emerson's ever expanding circle carries with it the spirit of enterprise capitalism in its endless search for the new: "The new continents are built out of the ruins of an old planet; the new races fed out of the decomposition of the foregoing. New arts destroy the old. See the investment of capital in aqueducts made useless by hydraulics; fortifications, by gunpowder; roads and canals, by railways; sails, by steam; steam by electricity."[4] Melville's "line of flight," however, is an escape from the cultural logic of expansive circularity. His journey into the Pacific does not enlarge the horizon—Emerson's second circle, after the transparent eyeball—but he has "crossed the line of horizon," becoming the Other. Ahab's magic circle of collection is also the opposite of the Emersonian emblem because the self-enclosing stasis of Ahab's magic circle short-circuits the profitability desire of the Emersonian emblem. The whirlpool created by the sinking of the *Pequod* is especially descriptive of the deadly inward pull, rather than outward expansion, of circles to the point of self-annihilation: "then all collapsed" (*MD* 572).

In this chapter about Melville's Pacific becoming, I choose not to write about scenes from *Typee,* a book that yields much more easily to the thematization of the Pacific. Instead, I want to focus on *Moby-Dick* and describe some of its formal features symptomatic of a book that is profoundly about the Pacific by failing to provide a coherent narrative of the oceanic space. I will look at Melville's interest in fancy, as opposed to imagination, as the method of writing, and at his penchant for the materiality of words, treating them as collectibles and subjecting them to the fate of visual, alphabetic interconnectedness rather than the predetermination of a master plot that foregrounds a romantic, self-reliant character. In other words, I am trying to read Melville against the grain of Emersonian imperial imagination by drawing attention not to what Melville says thematically but to how he says it—how his errant, digressive line of flight punctures the Emersonian circle. Melville's Pacific becoming, in my reading, becomes above all a linguistic one and anticipates the kind of counterpoetics I will describe in Part Three of the book.

Fancy

It may be fair to say that Melville is a literary scavenger in the South Seas. Like his commercial counterparts, Melville digs deep into the enduringly rich literary source in the Pacific and tries to convert his exotic life experiences into stories with the hope of earning the status of author and an income for living. To use Hershel Parker's words, as a whaleman Melville has "participated in one of the most remarkable literary phenomena of his time, the frontier-training of untutored writers."[5] Famous trainees in this regard include James Fenimore Cooper, Mark Twain, Jack London, and John Steinbeck, to name just a few. But the analogy between a commercial and a literary scavenger may not go too far. Especially in Melville's case, although he did try to make a living as an author by writing at least three books (*Typee, Omoo,* and *Mardi*) based to some extent on his Pacific experience, he had a very ambivalent view of the literary market. As Renker puts it, Melville "associated popular books with apparent meanings suited to the superficial skimmer of pages, and unpopular books with deep truths suited to 'men who *dive*,' thought-divers who come up with bloodshot eyes."[6] In his letter of October 6, 1849, to Lemuel Shaw, Melville confesses, "So far as I am individually concerned, & independent of my pocket, it is my earnest desire to write those sort of books which are said to 'fail.'"[7] As a literary scavenger, Melville is essentially an antiquarian collector who abhors representational exchange predicated on abstracting values from things or referents from words. To him, scavenging, collecting, and/or copying define a writer who is more or less skeptical of the economy of exchange, the idea of progress, and the romance of authorship.

Like Noah's Ark, Noah Webster's *An American Dictionary of the English Language* is a prototype of collections. It is, as Melville puts it, a vessel that "hold[s]" words; and he calls it "Noah Webster's Ark." In writing *Moby-Dick* and his other books, Melville struggles to follow the spelling adopted by the Webster dictionary, of which he has purchased at least three copies.[8] Sometimes he prides himself in having *collected* arcane items not found in this ark, words like *gam, squilgee, specksynder,* and *slobgollion;* and sometimes he abides by Webster's collection almost to the extent of foregoing the kind of authorial freedom advocated by Romanticism. In a letter to his British publisher John Murray on January 28, 1849, Melville writes, "It would form part of our agreement, also, that your edition is to be an exact transcript of the copy forwarded you;—unless, you should see fit to alter the spelling of a few words (spelt according to Webster) in conformity with some other standard." Although Melville immediately adds, "I swear by no particular creed in orthography," still he acknowledges, "my printers here 'go for' Webster."[9] Although Webster is important to Melville as a standard for orthography, it is also crucial as a collection of materials or a structure of a world out of which Melville has designed his own.

As Renker demonstrates in remarkable detail, Melville's composition is often based on phonetic approximations of words. In *Confidence Man*, for instance, "the text's graphic effects . . . manipulate and vary the constant syllable *char*, from which spring the words *charity, Charlie, Charlemont, charming, charlatan,* and *character,* all of which appear frequently," and *char* also "provides one subtle motivation for Melville's choice of the eccentric name 'China Aster', a near-acrostic for *character.*"[10] James William Nechas provides another important piece of evidence that Melville's composition often draws on the materiality of words: for instance, the title of Chapter 4, "The Counterpane," in *Moby-Dick* plays on the pun for the other two etymologically related words, "counterpoint" and "counterpart." It is in this chapter that Melville forces the reader to accept the contrapuntal relationship of Ishmael and Queequeg and to realize that they are counterparts only as human beings, a theme that is crucial to the book.[11]

What neither Renker nor Nechas has pointed out, however, is that such sequences of words approximate the way a dictionary is constructed. To find a collected item in a dictionary, Melville says, you sometimes need to "wear out your index-finger running up and down the columns" (*MD* 240), perhaps as physically as Queequeg counts pages. Words identified in this way bring out what lie next to them according to the alphabetic order, an order that, like an antiquarian's collection, dispenses with other sequences such as narrative linearity or plot structure. Melville's tendency to violate the latter two laws of fiction writing is quite notorious. The early, contemporary reviewers constantly complained about his seeming inability to tell a straight story. But Melville seemed quite determined to follow other laws of writing, other orders of arranging words. In a crucial chapter ("Young America in Literature") of *Pierre,* Melville announces that

among the various conflicting modes of writing history, there would seem to be two grand practical distinctions, under which all the rest must subordinately range. By the one mode, all contemporaneous circumstances, facts, and events must be set down contemporaneously; by the other, they are only to be set down as the general stream of the narrative shall dictate; for matters which are kindred in time, may be very irrelative in themselves. I elect neither of these; I am careless of either; both are well enough in their way; I write precisely as I please.[12]

Here the statement "I write precisely as I please" is much less a declaration of Romantic autonomy than a pronouncement on his disaffection with grand narrative principles advocated by both Romanticist writers and historians. Like Ishmael, Pierre shows in his work a deliberate carelessness, which, Melville believes, originates in Pierre's "poetic nature."[13] That Melville himself later completely gave up fiction writing and concentrated instead on poetry has been interpreted by Melvilleans as a logical step in his writerly trajectory, as a natural outcome of what Nina Baym has called Melville's "quarrel with fiction."[14] Although some critics have suggested that Melville "turned to poetry as an instrument of meditation rather than for the sake of melody or linguistic play,"[15] it is surely plausible that Melville's skepticism regarding fiction's truth-telling capacity can be attributed to a sustained obsession with the ontological status of language, with the materiality and opacity of words. To understand the poetics of Melville's writing, then, we need to follow the trails of words assembled in a text not necessarily by the law of thematic coherence or narrative closure, but by the choice of an author who treats words like a collector does his cherished items.

It may well be a coincidence that in the Harper 1846 edition of the Webster, the word *antiquarian* is preceded immediately by *antipuritan* (see Fig. 8.1). But given what we have said about Ishmael's antiquarian approach to history, which is a critique of Puritan typological historiography, such a coincidence may acquire meanings that canonical literary criticism, based on principles of Enlightenment rationality, would be unwilling to accept.[16] Yet, the significance of the correlation of *antiquarian* and *antipuritan* looms even larger when, on the facing column of the same page of the Webster, in the exact mirror position of *antiquarian,* we find a word that bears the unbearable burden of history for Puritanism: *antinomian.*

It may be true that Melville himself never used the word *antinomian*, nor does he even like to use the term, given his Calvinist family background. But antinomianism is a hidden issue in Melville; its manifestations are

AN-TI-MOR'AL-IST, *n.* An opposer of morality.

AN-TI-MU'SI-€AL, *a.* Opposed to music; having no ear for music. *Amer. Review.*

AN-TI-NE-PHRIT'I€, *a.* Counteracting diseases of the kidneys.

AN-TI-NE-PHRIT'I€, *n.* A medicine that tends to remove diseases of the kidneys.

AN-TI-NŎ'MI-AN, *a.* [Gr. *αντι*, and *νομος*.] Against law; pertaining to the Antinomians.

AN-TI-NŎ'MI-AN, *n.* One of a sect who maintain, that, under the gospel dispensation, the law is of no use or obligation; or who hold doctrines which supersede the necessity of good works and a virtuous life.

AN-TI-NŎ'MI-AN-ISM, *n.* The tenets of Antinomians.

* AN'TI-NO-MIST, *n.* One who pays no regard to the law, or to good works.

* AN'TI-NO-MY, *n.* A contradiction between two laws, or between two parts of the same law.

AN-TI-O'CHI-AN, *a.* Pertaining to Antiochus, the founder of a sect of philosophers.

AN-TI-PÃ'PAL, *a.* Opposing popery.

AN-TI-PA-PIS'TIC, } *a.* Opposed to popery or papacy.
AN-TI-PA-PIS'TI-€AL, } *Jortin.*

AN-TI-PAR'AL-LEL, *a.* Running in a contrary direction. *Hammond.*

AN-TI-PAR-A-LYT'I€, *a.* Good against the palsy.

AN-TI-PAR-A-LYT'I€, *n.* A remedy for the palsy.

AN-TI-PA-THET'I€, } *a.* Having a natural contrarie-
AN-TI-PA-THET'I-€AL, } ty, or constitutional aversion to a thing.

AN-TI-PA-THET'I-€AL-NESS, *n.* The quality or state of having an aversion or contrariety to a thing.

AN-TIP'A-THOUS, *a.* Adverse. *Beaumont.*

AN-TIP'A-THY, *n.* [Gr. *αντι* and *παθος*.] 1. Natural aversion; instinctive contrariety or opposition in feeling; an aversion felt at the presence, real or ideal, of a particular object.—2. In *ethics*, antipathy is hatred, aversion or repugnancy; *hatred* to persons; *aversion* to persons or things; *repugnancy* to actions.—3. In *physics*, a contrariety in the properties or affections of matter, as of oil and water.

AN-TI-PAT-RI-OT'I€, *a.* Not patriotic; opposing the interests of one's country.

AN-TI-PE-DO-BAP'TIST, *n.* [Gr. *αντι*, *παις*, *παιδος*, and *βαπτιζω*.] One who is opposed to the baptism of infants.

AN-TI-PER-IS-TAL'TIC, *a.* Opposed to peristaltic; reverted.

AN-TI-PE-RIS'TA-SIS, *n.* [Gr. *αντι* and *περιστασις*.] The opposition of a contrary quality, by which the quality opposed acquires strength.

AN-TI-PER-IS-TAT'I€, *a.* Pertaining to antiperistasis.

AN-TI-PES-TI-LEN'TIAL, *a.* Counteracting contagion or infection.

AN-TI-PHLO-GIS'TIAN, *n.* An opposer of the theory of phlogiston.

AN-TI-PHLO-GIS'TI€, *a.* Counteracting heat or inflammation; tending to reduce arterial action; opposed to the doctrine of phlogiston.

AN-TI-PHLO-GIS'TI€, *n.* Any medicine or diet which tends to reduce inflammation, or the activity of the vital power.

AN'TI-PHON, *n.* The chant or alternate singing in choirs of cathedrals.

AN-TIPH'O-NAL, AN-TI-PHON'I€, or AN-TI-PHON'I-€AL, *a.* Pertaining to antiphony or alternate singing.

AN-TIPH'O-NA-RY, *n.* [Gr. *αντι* and *φωνη*.] A service book in the Catholic church.

AN-TIPH'O-NER, *n.* A book of anthems or antiphons. *Chaucer.*

AN-TIPH'O-NY, *n.* [Gr. *αντι* and *φωνη*.] 1. The answer of one choir to another, when an anthem or psalm is sung by two choirs; alternate singing. 2. A species of psalmody, when a congregation is divided into two parts, and each sings the verses alternately. 3. The words given out at the beginning of a psalm, to which both the choirs are to accommodate their singing. 4. A musical composition of several verses, extracted from different psalms.

AN-TIPH'RA-SIS, *n.* [Gr. *αντι* and *φρασις*.] The use of words in a sense opposite to their proper meaning.

AN-TI-PHRAS'TIC, } *a.* Pertaining to antiphrasis.
AN-TI-PHRAS'TI-€AL, } *Ash.*

AN-TI-PHRAS'TI-€AL-LY, *adv.* In the manner of an antiphrasis.

AN-TIP'O-DAL, *a.* Pertaining to the antipodes; having the feet directly opposite.

* AN'TI-PODE, *plu.* ANTIPODES, *n.* [Gr. *αντι*, and *πους*, *ποδος*.] One who lives on the opposite side of the globe, and, of course, whose feet are directly opposite to ours.

AN-TI-POI'SON, (an-te-poy'zn) *n.* An antidote for poison.

AN'TI-POPE, *n.* One who usurps the papal power, in opposition to the pope.

AN'TI-PORT, *n.* An outward gate or door.

AN-TI-PRE-LAT'I-€AL, *a.* Adverse to prelacy.

AN'TI-PRIEST, *n.* An opposer or enemy of priests.

AN-TI-PRIEST'€RAFT, *n.* Opposition to priestcraft.

AN-TI-PRIN'CI-PLE, *n.* An opposite principle.

AN-TI-PROPH'ET, *n.* An enemy or opposer of prophets.

* AN-TIP'TO-SIS, *n.* [Gr. *αντι* and *πτωσις*.] In *grammar*, the putting of one case for another.

AN-TI-PU'RI-TAN, *n.* An opposer of Puritans.

AN-TI-QUA'RI-AN, *a.* Pertaining to antiquaries, or to antiquity. As a noun, this is used for *antiquary*.

AN-TI-QUA'RI-AN-ISM, *n.* Love of antiquities.

AN'TI-QUA-RY, *n.* [L. *antiquarius.*] One who studies into the history of ancient things, as statutes, coins, medals, paintings, inscriptions, books and manuscripts, or searches for them, and explains their origin and purport; one versed in antiquity.

AN'TI-QUATE, *v. t.* [L. *antiquo.*] To make old, or obsolete; to make old in such a degree as to put out of use. Hence, when applied to *laws or customs*, it amounts to make void, or *abrogate.*

AN'TI-QUA-TED, *pp.* Grown old; obsolete; out of use; having lost its binding force by non-observance.

AN'TI-QUA-TED-NESS, *n.* The state of being old, or obsolete.

AN'TI-QUATE-NESS, *n.* The state of being obsolete.

AN-TI-QUA'TION, *n.* The state of being antiquated.

AN-TIQUE', (an-teek') *a.* [Fr.] 1. Old; ancient; of genuine antiquity. 2. Old, as it respects the present age, or a modern period of time; of old fashion. 3. Odd; wild; fanciful; more generally written *antic.*

AN-TIQUE', (an-teek') *n.* In *general*, any thing very old; but, in a *more limited sense*, the remains of ancient artists, as busts, statues, paintings and vases, the works of Grecian and Roman antiquity.

AN-TIQUE'NESS, (an-teek'nes) *n.* The quality of being ancient; an appearance of ancient origin and workmanship.

AN-TIQ'UI-TY, *n.* [L. *antiquitas.*] 1. Ancient times; former ages; times long since past. 2. The ancients; the people of ancient times; as, the fact is admitted by all *antiquity.* 3. Ancientness; great age; the quality of being ancient. 4. Old age. *Shak.* 5. The remains of ancient times. In this *sense* it is *usually or always plural.*

AN-TI-REV-O-LU'TION-A-RY, *a.* Opposed to a revolution; opposed to an entire change in the form of government. *Burke.*

AN-TI-REV-O-LU'TION-IST, *n.* One who is opposed to a revolution in government.

AN-TI-SAB-BA-TA'RI-AN, *n.* One of a sect who oppose the observance of the Christian Sabbath.

AN-TI-SA'BI-AN, *a.* Opposed or contrary to Sabianism, or the worship of the celestial orbs.

AN-TI-SA-€ER-DO'TAL, *a.* Adverse to priests.

AN-TIS'CIAN, } *n.* [L. *antiscii.*] In *geography*, the inhab-
AN-TIS'CIANS, } itants of the earth, living on different sides of the equator, whose shadows at noon are cast in contrary directions.

AN-TI-SCOR-BU'TIC, or AN-TI-SCOR-BU'TI-€AL, *a.* Counteracting the scurvy.

AN-TI-SCOR-BU'TIC, *n.* A remedy for the scurvy.

AN-TI-SCRIP'TU-RISM, *n.* Opposition to the Holy Scriptures. *Boyle.*

AN-TI-SCRIP'TU-RIST, *n.* One that denies revelation. *Boyle.*

† AN'TI-SCRIPT, *n.* Opposition in writing to some other writing.

AN-TI-SEP'TIC, *a.* [Gr. *αντι* and *σηπτος*.] Opposing or counteracting putrefaction.

AN-TI-SEP'TIC, *n.* A medicine which resists or corrects putrefaction.

AN-TI-SO'CIAL, *a.* Averse to society; that tends to interrupt or destroy social intercourse.

AN-TI-SPA-SIS, *n.* [Gr. *αντι* and *σπαω*.] A revulsion of fluids from one part of the body to another.

AN-TI-SPAS-MOD'I€, *a.* [Gr. *αντι* and *σπασμος*.] Opposing spasm; resisting convulsions; as anodynes.

AN-TI-SPAS-MOD'I€, *n.* A remedy for spasm or convulsions.

AN-TI-SPAS'TIC, *a.* Causing a revulsion of fluids or humors. *Johnson.*

AN-TI-SPLE-NET'I€, *a.* Good as a remedy in diseases of the spleen. *Johnson.*

AN-TIS'TA-SIS, *n.* [Gr. *αντι* and *στασις*.] In *oratory*, the defense of an action from the consideration that, if it had been omitted, something worse would have happened.

AN-TIS'TES, *n.* [L.] The chief priest or prelate.

AN-TIS'TRO-PHE, } *n.* [Gr. *αντι* and *στροφη*.] 1. In *gram-*
AN-TIS'TRO-PHY, } *mar*, the changing of things mutually depending on each other; reciprocal conversion. 2. Among the *ancients*, that part of a song or dance, before the altar, which was performed by turning from west to east, in opposition to the *strophe.*

---

* *See Synopsis.* MÖVE, BOOK, DÒVE;—BULL, UNITE.—€ as K; G as J; S as Z; CH as SH; TH as in *this.* † *Obsolete.*

Figure 8.1 Noah Webster, *An American Dictionary of the English Language* (1846), p. 41.

often indirect and yet potentially strong. The canon of Melville studies has identified several crucial antinomian motifs in Melville's works: Ahab's quarrel with God, Ishmael's mockery of Christianity, Pierre's choice of "Lucy or God," Billy Budd's striking back, and Bartleby's "I would prefer not to."[17] Melville himself calls *Moby-Dick* "a wicked book." And he responds with the emphatic "no, no, no" to Emerson's insinuation that a true poet lives a virtuous life. Emerson writes in the essay "The Poet":

> Hence a great number of such as were professionally expressors of Beauty, as painters, poets, musicians, and actors, have been more than others wont to lead a life of pleasure and indulgence; all but the few who received the true nectar; and, as it was a spurious mode of attaining freedom, as it was an emancipation not into the heavens, but into the freedom of baser places, they were punished for that advantage they won, by a dissipation and deterioration.

Melville marks these lines and adds a strong rebuff at the bottom of the page: "No, no, no.—Titan—did he deteriorate?—Byron?—did he[?]—Mr E. is horribly narrow here."[18] Melville's antinomian symptoms could have been described as having a Romantic character, for indeed the antinomian streak that runs through Romanticism has given currency to the term *Romantic Antinomianism*. But such a reading of Melville misses the crucial point that he is also an anti-Romantic.

An antinomian is a religious enthusiast; and an enthusiast, as Webster defines, is "one of elevated fancy."[19] In Romantic literary theory, fancy is considered a faculty inferior to imagination. Coleridge has provided us a classical Romanticist conception or devaluation of fancy:

> Fancy . . . has no other counters to play with but fixities and definites. The fancy is indeed no other than a mode of memory emancipated from the order of time and space; and blended with, and modified by that empirical phenomenon of the will which we express by the word CHOICE. But equally with the ordinary memory it must receive all its materials ready made from the law of association.[20]

To write in the manner of Romanticism is to draw on the power of imagination, not fancy. And imagination is "a repetition in the infinite mind of the eternal act of creation in the infinite I AM."[21] By contrast, to rely on fancy is to write by a selection of words that are ready-made materials and by a mnemonic so withdrawn to itself that it separates from the universal order of time and space. The specific mode of collection I have tried to describe so far seems to rely exactly on fancy. For to fancy, again says Coleridge, is to "*bring together* images dissimilar in the main by some one point or more of likeness distinguished," whereas to collect is "to assemble or *bring together*" persons or things according to the "law of association" rather than a transcendental idea.[22] In the first surviving mention Melville made of the composition of *Moby-Dick*, he told Richard Henry Dana, Jr., that "to cook the thing up, one must needs throw in a little *fancy*, which from the nature of the thing, must be ungainly as the gambols of the whales themselves. Yet I mean to give the truth of the thing, spite of this."[23]

Fate

To "throw in a little fancy," to allow meanings to emerge almost by accident or by fate from an entangled web of connection among words themselves, means to be an anti-Romantic. In the essay "Fate and Character," Walter Benjamin opposes fate to character, defining character as a Romantic concept. Fate, Benjamin believes, is a connection or a nexus of meaning in which the natural life in man is indiscriminately "coupled to cards as to planets." It is a weave or net of snaring threads in which the possibility of difference is destroyed. Such nondifference in weblike interconnectedness "corresponds to the natural condition of the living," or to "the demonic stage of human existence." Character, by contrast, cuts apart the knots of fate and allows a Romantic hero to rise from the realm of mythical and natural interconnectedness.[24] Emerson, in two essays that Melville read and annotated, one entitled "Fate" and the other "Character," also claims that character should overcome fate.[25] To Emerson, fate limits us as human beings and it is an organization "tyrannizing over character." But our character is "a latent power," which, when evoked, becomes "a poetic attempt to lift this mountain of Fate."[26] Character, in other words, is our self-reliance that helps us defeat the superstition of fate. By contrast, Melville seems to have stood the Romantic conception on its head. It is seen not only in Ishmael's somewhat half-hearted acceptance of what "those stage managers, the Fates" have in store for him (*MD* 7), but more importantly in Melville's dealing with the destiny of individual words in his text. By producing texts based on finite variations of a syllable like *char* or a thread of theme tied through words like *antinomian, antipuritan,* and *antiquarian,* Melville restores words to their natural connections among themselves and subjects them to the fate of a predetermined collection. Such fate cannot be completely overcome by a Romantic hero's or an author's arrogant claim to transcendence and autonomy.

But Emerson would think otherwise. In speaking of character as a Romantic quality, Emerson uses a startling example to show that when fate is subdued, a strong character or race will emerge as a victorious conqueror:

> Fate is unpenetrated causes. The water drowns ship and sailor, like a grain of dust. But learn to swim, trim your bark, and the wave which drowned it, will be cloven by it, and carry it, like its own foam, a plume and a power. The cold is inconsiderate of persons, tingles your blood, freezes a man like a dew-drop. But learn to skate, and the ice will give you a grateful, sweet, and poetic motion. The cold will brace your limbs and brain to genius, and make you foremost men of time. Cold and sea will train an imperial Saxon race, which nature cannot bear to lose, and, after cooping it up for a thousand years in yonder England, gives a hundred Englands, a hundred Mexicos. All the bloods it shall absorb and domineer: and more than Mexicos,—the secrets of water and steam, the spasms of electricity, the ductility of metals, the chariot of the air, the ruddered balloon are awaiting you.[27]

If, as it so often has been argued, nineteenth-century Romanticism dovetails with nationalism and imperialism, then anti-Romanticism in literature should also have a stake in cultural politics. Obviously Melville, as we shall see, is telling us very different "secrets of water and steam," secrets that serve as strong antidotes to Emersonian triumphalism.

Finis

As opposed to the ever expansive Emersonian circle, *Moby-Dick* ends with a description of another kind of circle. Ishmael tells us in the "Epilogue" that "the Fates ordained" him to take the place of a bowsman on that fatal day and he was dropped astern when the White Whale attacked:

> So, floating on the margin of the ensuing scene, and in full sight of it, when the half-spent suction of the sunk ship reached me, I was then, but slowly, drawn towards the *closing vortex.* When I reached it, it had subsided to a creamy pool. Round and round, then, and *ever contracting* towards the button-like black bubble at the axis of that slowly *wheeling circle,* like another Ixion I did revolve. Till, gaining that *vital*

centre, the black bubble upward burst; and now, liberated by reason of
its cunning spring, and, owing to its great buoyancy, rising with great
force, the coffin life-buoy shot lengthwise from the sea, fell over, and
floated by my side. (573; italics mine)

This "closing vortex," "wheeling circle," "vital centre," "ever contracting,"
sucks in everything but miraculously leaves Ishmael intact and spits out
a buoy to save him. Not only that, the Fates seem to have further pro-
tected him as he floats on: "The unharming sharks, they glided by as if
with padlocks on their mouths; the savage sea-hawks sailed with
sheathed beaks" (573).

Here one might feel tempted to compare Ishmael to the "imperial
Saxon race," which, according to Emerson, "nature cannot bear to lose"
and "after cooping it up for a thousand years in yonder England, gives a
hundred Englands, a hundred Mexicos." But the story Ishmael comes
back to tell is not one of the romance but the disaster of imperial conquest: "Then all collapsed, and the great shroud of the sea rolled on as it
rolled five thousand years ago" (572). At the beginning of Part Two of
this book, I quote Melville saying, when he sobers up from his short-
lived ecstasy over entering the Pacific: "A moment of consideration will
teach that however baby man may brag of his science and skill, and
however much, in a flattering future, that science and skill may augment; yet for ever and for ever, to the crack of doom, the sea will insult
and murder him, and pulverize the stateliest, stiffest frigate he can
make" (273). Yet, in Melville's universe the *Pequod* is but one knot in a
chain of signifiers for such mighty fleets that cannot escape from the
doom. *Moby-Dick* was based on the disaster of the whaler *Essex;* there
was an eponymous frigate of the U.S. Navy, which was glorified in a
South American war but was later wrecked at sea; Melville came back
from the South Seas by way of a ship named the *United States,* and a few
years later when he used that experience to write *White-Jacket,* he gave
the man-of-war an ironic name, *Neversink.* With this vast collection of
ships, the Fates repeat again and again the lesson: "The masterless ocean
overruns the globe" (274).

But the most profound story Ishmael has come back to tell us is his
inability to tell a coherent story. If the Emerson brand of imperial imagination features a poet who is a seer, a namer, and a self-reliant character
overcoming the tyranny of fate, Melville's addiction to fancy and fate

dooms him to a giant stutter that ends *Moby-Dick:* "FINIS" (573). *Finis,* a Latin word for "end," is not really the end of Melville's book. Comprising "fins," the word denotes the parts, of both the fish and the book (Moby Dick and *Moby-Dick*), that are still alive, out there, fluttering, lingering, haunting. Read backwards, the word becomes "sin if." Sin if . . . Either a sacrilegious warning or an antinomian challenge, the word creates a circle within the book, a circle that is not an ever expansive ring, endlessly reaching for the new, but the "ever contracting" vortex, in which all collapse: the ship, the enterprise, the conquest, the structure and meaning of the word, and, above all, the narrative. Such has become Melville's Pacific becoming: the fins that flutter, taking up lives of their own; the sin of taking the flight of fancy, the line of flight, away from the narrative by pointing back to it, away from the circle of horizon by double-crossing it: first crossing by leaving, second crossing by puncturing.

Sometimes fiction can make a claim on history. Melville's closing vortex in the Pacific Ocean reemerged a century later in the shape of another destructive circle: a nuclear mushroom. Close to where the fictional *Pequod* went down (off the coast of Bikini Island), the United States conducted its first offshore testing of nuclear weapons in 1946 and exploded its first hydrogen bomb in 1954, a series of events that signify both the U.S. apotheosis in the Pacific region and the horror of destruction that characterizes much of Pacific history. It is against such a backdrop of violence in history and of History that I will now turn to the next chapters, where in the work of counterpoetics history is interrogated for its fictionality and fiction attempts to reclaim its historicity.

PART THREE

Counterpoetics:
Islands, Legends, Maps

Transpacific geopolitics lies at the heart of Asian American history. The very beginnings of modern Asian America, as David Palumbo-Liu has pointed out, may be given context within a respatialization of the nation: the United States' annexation of the Philippines and Hawaii, its interest in the Sino-Japanese War, its war in the Pacific, its concern with China's and Taiwan's position in the Cold War, its wars in Korea and Indochina, have all affected Asian Americans profoundly.[1] Curious enough, the more entangled the United States is in the Asian-Pacific region, the more segregationist its internal spatial practice becomes. Angel Island and Japanese internment during World War II are two prime examples of such segregationist spatialization. If Angel Island represents modern America's attempt to manage its racial frontier along the Pacific coast by preventing the encroachment of unwanted bodies into its national space, the internment of Japanese Americans may also be understood as a spatial practice of dissecting America's transpacific routes by relocating or uprooting a people who have come across the Pacific. Like the detaining station on Angel Island, these internment camps were "worlds of their own, extraterritorial spaces of liminality and statelessness."[2] By consigning a people of transpacific roots to such bracketed spaces, America redefines itself through deterritorialization. In his otherwise brilliant reading of Asian American history through the concept of spatiality, Palumbo-Liu focuses, however, mostly on America's macromanagement of its racial frontier. By contrast, in this part of my book I am interested more in Asian American micro-resistance, imaginary crossing, and poetic reterritorialization.

9

The Poetics of Error: Angel Island

The black Africans who survived the dreaded "Middle Passage" from the west coast of Africa to the New World did not sail alone. Violently and radically abstracted from their civilizations, these Africans nevertheless carried with them to the Western hemisphere aspects of their cultures that were meaningful, that could not be obliterated, and that they chose, by acts of will, not to forget: their music, their myths, their expressive institutional structures, their metaphysical systems of order, and their forms of performance . . . At that liminal crossroad of culture contact and ensuing difference . . . Africa meets Afro-America.

—Henry Louis Gates, Jr., *The Signifying Monkey*

In the translation . . . lies the disappeared history of distinctions in another space . . . full of the movements of languages and peoples still in historical sedimentation at the bottom, waiting for the real virtuality of our imagination.

—Gayatri Chakravorty Spivak, *Death of a Discipline*

Within the horizons of the historical and literary imaginations of Mark Twain, Henry Adams, Liang Qichao, and Herman Melville, the colored bodies that move across the Pacific register different significations. To Twain, they are indispensable for the booming of California and the cultivation of Hawaii; to Adams, they would, like the "furtive Yacoob and Ysaac" coming from the Atlantic, create a decentering effect on his unity of history; to Liang, they are an anomaly to his nationalist vision because they have moved away from the body of nation; and to Melville, they are "renegades, castaways, and cannibals" who staff the whaling ships. But just like the stuttering Queequeg and Ahab's silent secret crew, they are what Gayatri Chakbravorty Spivak once called the subalterns who cannot speak.[1] In other words, although their transpacific displacements have opened a window to the new vistas of global geopolitics, they are rarely considered in canonical literature as agents of historical change.

Angel Island poetry, however, tells a very different story. Written on the walls of the wooden barracks of the detaining station on Angel Island off the coast of San Francisco, these poems delineate historical trajectories that are in many ways unaccountable in canonical discourses. They belie the pitfalls of teleological History by virtue of their modes of inscription. In this chapter I will describe these specific modes of inscription, their inherent subversive poetics, and their imbrication with marginalized forms of historical imagination. I want to look at these poems as examples of *tibishi* (poetry inscribed on the wall), a traditional Chinese form of travel writing that provides an outlet for the large social sector that is denied the right to write history. Seen by its cultural function, tibishi in the case of Angel Island poetry becomes indistinguishable from graffiti, a scriptural practice that is sometimes condemned as vandalism and at other times commissioned as artwork. Not understanding the scriptural economy of these poems has led to a reductive hermeneutics in the hitherto efforts of transcribing, translating, and interpreting them. This kind of hermeneutics may sit well with an economic system that favors productive abstraction and with a political system that recognizes only fully fledged citizen-subjects, but it lies at odds with what I call the poetics of error. Characterized by misspellings, misattributions, and mistranslations, the poetics of error in these poems has significant linguistic, historical, and cross-cultural implications. Read differently, misspellings spell out linguistic nonconformity and the fictionality of standard orthography, misattributions can be attributed to folk revisions of authorized history and intentional conflations of cultural origins, and mistranslations translate code-switching and heteroglossia. Understood this way, the poetics of error echoes the liminality as well as subversity of the anonymous poets' status in a world delineated by expansionist or nationalist historiography.

The discovery of what we now call Angel Island poems is a remarkable story:

The Chinese detention barrack on Angel Island, a two-story wood building located on a hill overlooking San Francisco Bay, stood abandoned for more than two decades until it was finally marked by the government for destruction. In 1970, park ranger Alexander Weiss noticed characters inscribed on the walls inside and concluded they were writings left by Chinese immigrants once detained there for questioning. Weiss informed his superiors but they did not share his enthusiasm or belief in the significance of the calligraphy on the walls. Weiss contacted Dr. George Araki of San Francisco State University, who along with San Francisco photographer Mak Takahashi went out to the island and photographed practically every inch of the barrack walls that bore writing, most of which was poetry. Their discovery soon sparked enough local Asian American community interest to lobby for its preservation, and in 1976 the Legislature appropriated $250,000 for the preservation of the building.[2]

As a result, more than one hundred and thirty-five calligraphic poems have survived. But the exact number is impossible to tell, partly because many of the poems are barely legible and have thus not been transcribed, and partly because the transcribers do not always agree as to where one poem ends and another begins on the wall.[3] Such a feature of textual instability actually pertains to one of the most important literary genres in which history and writing remain entangled: Chinese travel writing.

I modify the otherwise generic term *travel writing* by adding "Chinese" in order to emphasize the specificity of this literary tradition in China, the specificity of the Chinese travelogue's uneasy relation to historical writing as determined by the particular politics of Chinese historiography. Throughout imperial China, historical writing was subject to the court's authorization and domination. Only court-appointed historians were allowed to write and publish "history." The private compilation of historical facts in book format often led to imprisonment or other forms of physical punishment of the unauthorized historian. Travel writing thus provides an important outlet for writers who desire to make historical references but are forbidden to produce what may be deemed as historical accounts. The sites that the writers visit, be they relics, ruins, monuments, or natural resorts, are usually haunted by historical memories. A visit to these sites triggers some thoughts on the writer's part, thoughts that are historical comments in essence but disguised as random observations of a traveler. Take, for instance, the following four-line poem by the famous Tang poet Du Mu (803–852):

PASSING THE HUAQING PALACE

Piles of embroidery seen afar from Chang'an,
mountain-top a thousand gates open one by one.
A steed above the red dust, a concubine smiling,
no one knows it's the litchi coming.[4]

The Huaqing Palace was a well-known entertainment place for the Ming emperor of the Tang dynasty and his concubine, Yang Guifei. The emperor's obsession with his *femme fatale* almost ruined the dynasty, and he was forced by his rebellious army to order her suicide. Notorious for doting on his concubine, the emperor set up a special express delivery route all the way from Canton in the south to the capital, Chang'an, in the north (an ancient Chinese version of today's Fedex) in order to bring her fresh litchi, which grew only in the south. Unmistakably embedded in this poem is the poet's severe criticism of the emperor's debauchery and corruption, and this poem constitutes in essence a historical comment on a previous reign of the dynasty. But the criticism is couched within a poem, and the severity of historical commentary is camouflaged by a title that gives an almost casual, occasional feeling: "*Passing* the Huaqing Palace." "Passing" designates the poem as an incidental piece, a vignette of travelogue, which is generically differentiated from historical writing. But in an atmosphere in which historical writing is tightly controlled, the travelogue provides a tool for the writer to comment on history. As Richard E. Strassberg puts it in his study of Chinese travel writing, "When a traveler adopted the narrative persona of the historian, he was appropriating a potent form of literary authority."[5] The potency comes from the inherent authority of history and from the fact that it is historical commentary disguised as travel writing: history *passing* for travelogue.

The tantalizing relation between history and travelogue is reincarnated in the body of Angel Island poetry. Needless to say, these poems, composed by detainees who were being interrogated in humiliating ways, occupy a most marginal cultural space. Their three-decade-long existence in complete oblivion before coming to light on the brink of destruction testifies to their marginality and fragility. But just as travel writing seems marginal within the Chinese literary canon but remains subversive in its function as alternative history, Angel Island poems demonstrate the tenacity with which the powerless take advantage of the power of writing and inscribe themselves into the fabric of history, or rather, tear the fabric apart. For us to recapture this tenacity, it is necessary to look at these poems not only as Chinese travel writing in general but also as its special subgenre—題壁詩 (*tibishi*).

Literally "poetry inscribed on the wall," tibishi has been an important form of composing and disseminating poems in Chinese literary history. The space for inscription is actually not limited to "walls"; poems written on cliffs, rocks, doors, windows, rafters, and even snow fields also belong to this genre. At inns and roadside pavilions, where travelers usually stop for a rest, special kinds of "poetry boards" were even set up for the convenience of the poetically inspired.[6]

On the walls of the wooden barracks where the Chinese immigrants were detained, there were no "poetry boards," although the sense of transition one felt at a modern-day detaining station was surely as strong as at the roadside pavilions of ancient times. The poetic desire thus inspired was equally deep. The detainees carved poems with knives and used brushes to paint them over so that the words would be legible. Many of these poems self-consciously address themselves and the others as tibishi:

> Over a hundred poems are on the walls.
> Looking at them, they are all pining at the delayed progress.
> (*Island* 62–63)

Or,

> There are tens of thousands of poems composed on these walls.
> They are all cries of complaint and sadness. (66–67)

And they are all meant to be read by the other detainees who will stand exactly on the same spots where the poems were composed and who share the same experiences of incarceration, frustration, and humiliation:

> Let this be an expression of the torment which fills my belly.
> Leave this as a memento to encourage fellow souls. (121–122)

Or,

> My fellow villagers seeing this should take heed and remember,
> I write my wild words to let those after me know. (162–163)

This feature of tibishi, in calling attention to writing as set on something (the wall) and absorbed in its material relations to its intended readers, raises questions about the politics of transcription and reading.

Undoubtedly, as the editors of the first comprehensive anthology, *Island: Poetry and History of Chinese Immigrants on Angel Island, 1910–1940*, have declared, these poems "express the thoughts of the individuals who wrote them" (31). For instance, the anonymous poet's frustration over being detained and sense of disappointment are evident in the opening poem of the anthology:

> The sea-scape resembles lichen twisting and turning for a
>   thousand li.
> There is no shore to land and it is difficult to walk.
> With a gentle breeze I arrived at the city thinking all would
>   be so.
> At ease, how was one to know he was to live in a wooden
>   building? (34–35)

Or, as in another poem, the sadness is expressed in simple and clear language:

> The insects chirp outside the four walls.
> The inmates often sigh.
> Thinking of affairs back home,
> Unconscious tears wet my lapel. (54–55)

Apparently, these poems in translation pose little challenge to English readers. In apoliticized aesthetic terms, these are what Sau-Ling C. Wong would call "artlessly direct" poems whose significance would have to derive, as she insists, from their contents alone.[7] But the illusion of their transparency, one might suggest, is created by the editors' disregard for the modes of inscription of these poems. In the "Translators' Notes," the editors/translators, like Wong, make clear their preference of the thematic content to the formal materiality of the poems:

> The form [in our translation] is oftentimes compromised in order to
> retain the content, which we for historical reasons feel is our first pri-
> ority. We do not claim adherence to the poets' original meters or
> rhyme-schemes. By imitating the poetic structure, we feel an injustice
> to the meaning of the poem would have been committed. (31)

What are the "historical reasons," and what is the "meaning of the poem"? The historical reasons that they have in mind likely refer to the political urgency of publishing a body of ethnic writing that has been historically underrepresented. These are undoubtedly "historical" records, and important ones at that. But in choosing content over form, the editors seem to have forgotten to consider the particular ways in which these poems, as tibishi, pose a threat to canonical historical narratives: their inscription resists hermeneutic containment.[8]

Take the following poem, for instance:

> In January I started to leave for Mexico.
> Passage reservations delayed me until mid-autumn.
> I had wholeheartedly counted on a quick landing at the city,
> But the year's almost ending and I am still here in this building.
>   (*Island* 167)

Except for being a simple narrative of the poet's long delayed journey, what else does the poem say, or what is the meaning of this poem? The editors relegate this poem to the "Appendix" of the anthology, perhaps because the poem says almost nothing significant; it expresses some frustration, but the frustration lacks the kind of thematic intensity found in other poems. Here we could resort to the notion of "minority literature," as propagated by Gilles Deleuze and Felix Guattari, the notion that language in minority writing stops being "representative" and that its poetic and political efficacy comes more from the physicality and opacity of the language than from the transparency of its semantics.[9] But we would have to apply the French theory advisedly. As Masao Miyoshi reminds us, "Genres, like most other things, are specific to history and geography."[10]

By demonstrating the embeddedness of Angel Island poetry in the Chinese literary tradition, my hope is precisely to foreground the importance of knowing the contingent origin of cultural practices in our study of transnational literature, the necessity of recognizing, as Miyoshi puts it, "the form's native visage and lineage."[11] In other words, to have a better view of the liminal crossroads of culture at which Angel Island poetry stands, we need to know not only the historical facts of Chinese immigration to the United States, but also the Chinese literary tradition out of which this poetry has originated and against which the poetry must be interpreted. I put "contingent" before the word "origin" because such an origin *is* contingent: ultimately, the poetry transgresses and unsettles the boundaries of that origin, those nationalist historical frameworks. But for now let me stay, if only for a moment, within the confines of Chinese poetics and try to explain how we should read the simple poem just encountered, a poem that seems to have nothing to say.

Our problem lies precisely in the word "say." In the confines of the present work, it is impossible to unfold the full array of connotations of this simple term, connotations ranging from the Taoist notion of "Tao is unsayable" to Heidegger's *Sagen* or *Dichtung*. Instead, this discussion will be limited to the notion of 詩言志 (*shi yan zhi*), which ostensibly is the first Chinese definition of poetry and which has remained the key concept in classical Chinese literary criticism. Translated variously as "poetry says the mind," or "poetry expresses human nature," the statement proposes an expressive-affective conception of poetry, as opposed to the mimetic-representative conception in the Western tradition. "The poem is that to which what is intently on the mind goes," says the "Great Preface" to *The Book of Songs,* "In the mind its being intent; coming out in language, it is a poem."[12] Though sounding very much like the Wordsworthian notion that "Poetry is a spontaneous overflow of powerful feelings," the Chinese conception is actually based on a philosophical tradition significantly different from that on which Romanticism was predicated and with which Romanticism had struggled. The key difference is that between the Chinese monistic world-view and Western dualism: whereas Chinese believe that the cosmic principle or Tao "is totally immanent in this world, and there is no suprasensory realm that lies beyond, is superior to, or is different in kind from the level of physical beings," the Western tradition proposes a dichotomy of exterior phenomena and interior or transcendental essence.[13]

If this schematization of the philosophical difference sounds crude and simplistic—admittedly it is[14]—the divergence between the consequent views of poetry may be more specific: "poem," with its Greek roots in *poiêma* and *poein* (to make), suggests an object made, an outside separated from an inside; by contrast, *shi*, the Chinese word for poetry or poem, is not an object made by the writer but IS the writer. As Stephen Owen points out, *shi yan zhi* may well be a tautological statement. The word 詩 (*shi*) consists of 言 (*yan*) and 寺 (*si*); if we interpret the latter component as 志 (*zhi*) by a pseudo-etymology as well as homophony, then the Chinese statement merely repeats itself internally, without giving a real definition of poetry, just as the Greek statement tautologizes itself: "A poem ('to make') is a thing made."[15] Hence, we may legitimately interpret *shi yan zhi* as meaning "poetry says," with a stress on the intransitive verb, just as Heidegger has emphasized *saying* in philosophical hermeneutics. This emphasis, not on something out there to be represented by a poem, but on the act of saying itself brings us back to the aforementioned Angel Island poem, which seems to say nothing.

The fact that the anonymous poet has given us very little to work with in reading his poem only foregrounds the greater fact that he wrote a poem on the wall, tried to express some feelings, and left traces of himself. This is not to collapse literature with sociology ("not that there's anything wrong with it"), but to suggest that one of the significant ways literature acquires its social function is through its modes of inscription. A poem inscribed on the walls of a detention center by an inmate in that particular context need not, in some ways, say much in order to be historically effective. It may sound strange to put the matter this way, but such a poem, as tibishi, which in turn provides a marginalized form of historical writing, challenges us to confront the material properties of the graphic space. If the existence of masterpieces in literary history relies explicitly or implicitly on the notion of an abstracted and infinitely transmissible text, tibishi calls this notion into question. It seems that these poems achieve their efficacy more through their physical traces than by being beyond these traces; they draw our attention to the act of their saying and not merely to what they say. This feature puts them in close alliance with another form of writing that is often criminalized but resists political/thematic containment—graffiti.

When labeled as vandalism, graffiti constitute a crime of writing. By means of defacement, they intentionally violate property rights. "They draw attention to themselves," writes Dick Hebdige, "They are an expression both of impotence and a kind of power—the power to disfigure."[16] As such, graffiti exhibit, in the words of Susan Stewart, "a stylization inseparable from the body, a stylization that, in its impenetrable 'wildness', could surpass even linguistic reference and serve purely as the concrete evidence of an individual existence and the reclamation of the environment through the label of the personal."[17] When conceived as artwork, however, graffiti join the ranks of commodity and lose their signature of cultural resistance. The so-called tags, which used to provide clues for the police to track down and crack down inveterate vandals, have now become signatures of commodifiable authenticity. The history of collecting, editing, and anthologizing tibishi shows a similar process of personalization and depersonalization, legitimization and delegitimization. Poems by canonical authors are often copied and preserved, whereas poems by anonymous authors get ignored and erased. Hence, canonization of tibishi is also a process of commodification that changes the nature of the scriptural economy associated with "writing on the wall," relocating traces of inscription from the site of destructive "doodling" to the domain of productive labor.

As we saw earlier, Angel Island poems were on the brink of destruction because the park ranger's superiors considered them as meaningless graffiti. (The task of maintaining a public park consists, let me remind you, of erasing from public space unauthorized inscriptions and erecting in the same space signs of utter oxymoron, such as "DO NOT WRITE ON WALLS.") The process of transcribing and publishing these poems is inevitably in danger of replicating the process of legitimization and delegitimization, which the original inscriptions have questioned with their defiant opacity, with their status as vandalistic graffiti and not just reproducible poems with recuperable themes and thoughts. The potency and efficacy of these poems thus come from their form rather than their content, from their occupying an ambivalent space between a form of vandalism to be condemned and a form of historical record to be preserved. That ambivalence is what the earlier efforts of transcribing, translating, and publishing these poems have missed.

Perhaps as appropriate to the ambivalence, these poems also carry out nonstandard linguistic practices, ranging from misspellings to incorrect uses of phrases, ungrammatical sentences, uses of vernacular, neologisms that result from imperfect translations, and incorrectly attributed references. Mikhail Bakhtin would have celebrated all these features as "heteroglossia," features that he has attributed almost exclusively to novels but that actually abound in other carnivalesque genres such as folk narratives, graffiti, and tibishi.

In the published editions, the transcribers and editors of Angel Island poetry painstakingly try to "correct" the somewhat corrupted texts that do not follow standard linguistic practices. The notes to the Chinese version of the poems in the anthology are full of "errata," which identify the original errors that have since been "corrected." One "factual error" identified by the editors appears in this poem, entitled "Inscription about a Wooden Building:

> A building does not have to be tall; if it has windows,
>   it will be bright.
> Island is not far, Angel Island.

Alas, this wooden building disrupts my
    travelling schedule.
Paint on the four walls are green,
And green is the grass which surrounds.
It is noisy because of the many country folk,
And there are watchmen guarding during the night.
To exert influence, one can use a square-holed
    elder brother.
There are children who disturb the ears,
But there are no incoherent sounds that cause fatigue.
I gaze to the south at the hospital,
And look to the west at the army camp.
This author says, "What happiness is there in this?"

The editors' note reads: "The writer here appears to be confused in his directions. The long axis of the barracks building runs roughly in an eastern-western direction. The occupants can see the hospital to the north from windows in the building's north wall. Looking east, the Ft. McDowell buildings can be seen. No building can be seen from the south wall windows which face the hillside" (*Island* 70).

As the editors have correctly noted, this poem imitates "Loushi Ming" ("Inscription about a Humble House") by the famous Tang poet Liu Yuxi (A.D. 772–842). For the sake of comparison, let me put Liu's poem alongside the Chinese version of this Angel Island poem (see Figs. 9.1 and 9.2). As we see, the Angel Island poem follows Liu's poem closely by replicating some of the key words and the rhyme schemes: *ming, qing, ding, xing,* and *you*. The eighth line, which the editors believe to have indicated confusion in direction, duplicates the two directional words in Liu's poem: *nan* (south) and *xi* (west). As I said earlier, a crucial feature of Chinese travel writing is that it enables marginalized, unauthorized writers to inscribe themselves into the fabric of history. As Liu's poem is one of the paragons of Chinese literary classics, the anonymous Angel Island poet's effort to imitate closely is evidently an attempt to appropriate the kind of authority embodied in Liu's poem. Compared with intertextual references that transmit textual efficacy and authority, facts such as what lies in which direction in one's vision may seem of less significance.

Viewed differently, however, the seemingly trivial factual reference played a crucial part in these detainees' lives. The poetics of error was

陋室銘

山不在高，有仙則名；
水不在深，有龍則靈。
斯是陋室，唯吾德馨。
苔痕上階綠，草色入帘青。
談笑有鴻儒，往來無白丁。
可以調素琴，閱金經。
無絲竹之亂耳，無案牘之勞形。
南陽諸葛盧，西蜀子雲亭。
孔子雲："何陋之有？"

Figure 9.1 Liu Yuxi, "Inscriptions about a Humble House."

actually a dangerous drama that they lived and performed every day. As we know, most of them were detained as a result of the 1882 Chinese Exclusion Act, which effectively banned legal immigration of Chinese laborers and allowed only family-based immigration in addition to a few other categories. Many of these detainees were the so-called paper sons—they claimed to be descendants of a native-born U.S. citizen. According to historians, the paper-son scheme began in the 1880s when Chinese merchants brought over fake sons. In the 1890s, Chinese began taking advantage of the Fourteenth Amendment, which grants citizenship to anyone born in the United States and their foreign-born children. Villages in Southern China developed a sophisticated paper-son slot system and sent over thousands of people every year to claim nativity in the United States. Such a wide-scale immigration fraud led one federal judge to comment in 1901, "if

木屋銘

樓不在高，有窗則明；
島不在遠，煙治埃崙。
嗟此木屋，阻我行程。
四壁油漆綠，週圍草色靑。
喧譁多鄉里，守夜有巡丁。
可以施運動，孔方兄。
有孩子之亂耳，無咕嗶之勞形。
南望醫生房，西瞭陸軍營。
作者雲：　"何樂之有？"

Figure 9.2 Angel Island, "Inscription about a Wooden Building."

the story told in the courts were true, every Chinese woman who was in the United States twenty-five years ago must have had at least 500 children."[18] In order to stop the trend, immigration officers who interviewed the Chinese applicants covered family history, relationships, village life, and other matters that should be of common knowledge to the applicant and his witnesses, a procedure that the Angel Island detainees would have had to go through. The detainees were regularly questioned about a wealth of legally irrelevant minutiae, as the following transcript shows:

Q: How many houses are there on your row, the first one?
A: Three. One of them is tumbled down.
Q: Which one is that?
A: The third one of the last one of the row.

Q: Who lives in the second one of your row?

A: Mah Sin Ick.

Q: What does he do?

A: He is dead.

Q: When did he die?

A: He died when I was a small boy.

Q: Did he leave a family?

A: Yes, he left two sons. His wife is dead also.

Q: When did she die?

A: I don't remember. She died long ago.

Q: What are the boys' names?

A: Mah Quock You, Mah Quock Him. I don't know the age of Quock You. Quock Him is over ten.

Q: Is the oldest one married?

A: No.

Q: Who takes care of them in that house?

A: The older brother has gone to Siam. The younger one is now working in Kung Yick village.

Q: Does anybody occupy that house?

A: No, it is empty.

Q: Then your house is the only house occupied on that row?

A: Yes.

Q: Who lives in the first house of the second row?

A: Mah Kong Kee.[19]

The same set of questions would be asked of each of the other applicants from the same village, and the answers would have to match, or all of them would be denied entry to the United States. Here, what Clifford Geertz would have called "local knowledge," as demanded by these questions, should remind us of the poem, "Inscription about a Wooden Building": What building lies in which direction?

Most of the applicants came with "coaching notes," which they had to remember by rote. The questions were so absurdly detailed and irrelevant that they sometimes even confused the "real" applicants and not the paper sons. Hence all potential immigrants, both the real and the fake, would have to rely on common coaching notes that provided them with detailed local knowledge about their village. In this case, errors were no longer factual but performative, a result of either incorrect memory of the coaching notes or successful acquisition of textual knowledge. Errors, then, were the thin ice on which every detainee on Angel Island would have to tread every day.

"Not to know that a hind had no horn," says Aristotle, "is a less serious matter than to paint it inartistically."[20] As opposed to empirical error, Aristotle suggests that artistic merit be the standard for evaluating a work of art, a standard that, as we know from his *Poetics,* gives value to poetry and a legitimate social position to poets, who may otherwise have been expelled from Plato's Republic. But graffiti, before being commodified and institutionalized, are not works of art. On the contrary, as Stewart remarks, graffiti "form a critique of the status of all artistic artifacts, indeed a critique of all privatized consumption, and carry out that threat in full view, in repetition, so that the public has nowhere to look, no place to locate an averted glance."[21] The so-called errors in Angel Island poems thus raise the question of where, if anywhere, we can locate securely our averted glance of hermeneutics, about whether regarding them as historical documents or literary texts whose efficacy derives mainly from their contents has actually deprived them of their unique mode of being historical.

This important question has been completely avoided in the ongoing canonization of these poems. Appearing in the *Heath Anthology of American Literature,* for instance, these poems are printed only in English translations.[22] Needless to say, in this monolingual version, the poetics of error is never an issue; instead, the poems are made to appear clean, conforming to the horizontal linearity of English poetry, and easy to understand with the help of footnotes. Indeed, they have become finished products ready for "privatized consumption," a hermeneutic practice that graffiti originally intend to unsettle. Thus, the translation unwittingly becomes a filtering process, eerily resembling procedures on Angel Island, where the detainees underwent medical examinations and interrogations, and were divided into categories of the admissible and the inadmissible. The irony is as deep as the errors are unmistakable.

10

Legends from Camp:
Lawson Fusao Inada

Japanese American poet Lawson Fusao Inada once spoke of his "personal" problem with the Pacific in a poem entitled "Shrinking the Pacific":

> The problem, as I see it, is *water.*
> Not that there's too much or too little of it—
>
> because there's always been exactly, precisely,
> just enough water to go around
> and around and up and down the world,
> again and again and again and again and again—
>
> but *where* it is has bearing on my existence.
> Now, this is simply my own personal perspective.

It is not the quantity of water that matters to the poet. "The Atlantic, of course," writes Inada later in the poem, "is just *gigantic*—/but, oh, well, that's their problem to deal with." It is the geographical location, the "where," that "has bearing on my existence." Calling the Atlantic "their problem" and taking on the Pacific as "my own," the poet goes on to "conduct a little experiment":

> I'll hold the world in my hands
> and, slowly, slowly, easily, appropriately,
> proceed to squeeze some land together,
> proceed to make some water move elsewhere,
> and, there, without inconveniencing anybody,
> I've gone and done it: Shrunk the Pacific.

What, one may ask, is the purpose of this experiment? The poet does not say explicitly, except that he goes on to describe a scene of increasing ease of transpacific travel after the shrinkage: with the new proximities of Sydney and Santiago, Manila and Acapulco, Canton and Mazatlan, Tokyo and San Francisco, and so on, one may easily drive to the Pacific coast, hop a ferry, fly a plane, or even take the bridge, and bop into and around Hokkaido for lunch; "Maybe one can stay the night, or come back to Oregon/Which, by now, is full of Hokkaido tourists."[1]

In his critique of Asia/Pacific as a space of cultural production, Rob Wilson suggests that Inada's poem describes the "compression of Pacific space-time," which recalls Mark Twain's earlier intuitions that "new technologies of travel, shipping, and communication will reshape global space . . . and allow the multifaced penetration of national interests into the Pacific."[2] Wilson's reading of the poem as Inada's critique of transpacific capitalism is certainly insightful, but there is another dimension to the poet's experiment on shrinking the Pacific. Given the curious contradiction between the increased involvement of the United States in the Pacific and its repeated spatial practice of bracketing or uprooting the transpacific people, Inada's recognition of the Pacific as his own problem and his attempt to shorten the oceanic distance may be symptoms of the poet's desire to reclaim the transpacific from nationalized interests and to reinscribe it as a space to invoke communal memory and minority survival. To understand this desire fully, we need to look at Inada's internment camp poems.

In the introduction to *Legends from Camp,* Inada links the internment camps directly to the American experience in the Pacific and to the long history of transpacific encounter:

> We've lived with the experience since—on a continual basis. And I've often wondered: What does it all mean? History offers clues: The *American* camps are part of the American experience, with many patterns and connections; also, there are international ramifications to consider, going back at least to President Fillmore in 1854, and the "opening" of Japan. (Actually, Columbus was heading to "Cipangu," Japan.)

Such a macro-view of history, despite its apparent advantage of reinscribing the transpacific into the American, creates a sense of alienation that the poet finds unsettling: "Still there's a remoteness to history, and to simply know the facts is not satisfactory. There is more to life than that."[3]

Just as in "Shrinking the Pacific" where he claims the Pacific as a personal and personalized problem, in this sequence of poems about the internment Inada tries over and over to shrink the distance, the "remoteness," between the history and us as readers.

The uncaptioned photo that opens the poetic sequence captures immediately the problem with historical knowledge (see Fig. 10.1). In this image, a little Asian boy looks out at us or at the camera with a painful grin on his face. Perhaps the sunlight, which comes from the direction of the camera or of us, is too bright for his eyes; or perhaps he is afraid of the soldier in his military cap, whom we cannot see directly in the picture but whose dark shadow is lying on the ground. The two shadows, the boy's and the soldier's, are so conspicuous that they resonate strongly with the sense of "remoteness" that the poet has attributed to history. Foreshadowing Theresa Cha's dissatisfaction with documentary history, which we will study in the next chapter, here Inada also attempts to change our relationship to history and tries to bridge the gap between the two types of history, as described by Michel de Certeau: "One type of history ponders what is comprehensible and what are the conditions of understanding;

Figure 10.1 Lawson Fusao Inada, *Legends from Camp,* p. 1.

the other claims to reencounter lived experience, exhumed by virtue of a knowledge of the past."[4] In Cha's *Dictee,* the tensions between the (im)possibilities for the reader to know and the poet to tell are dramatized by a scene of "stressed reading." In *Legends from Camp,* these tensions are first staged by shadows on the ground: The boy's shadow on the ground may very well be a position the poet has to occupy as he looks back to his own camp experience years later, looking at his old self in the picture, trying to tell "his" story; the soldier's shadow, as positioned in the image, could easily be the reader's if there were light coming from our back.[5] If the frame of the photo constitutes boundaries of a visual/virtual camp, the boy who is stuck inside may have a chance to let his life be known and his words heard if the readers can erase the distance, the remoteness, to the inside of the frame. In this case, the reader is implicated in history by his or her shadowy presence in the image, a presence that the grinning and innocent-looking boy or the poet has challenged us to acknowledge.

A shadow, however, designates both presence and absence. It is an index to something real as well as an icon of the lacuna—it points to the insurmountable distance between the absent object and its shadowy presence. Shadows or ghosts are deadly because they are alive or real ambiguously, neither here nor there. This ambiguity is further enacted in Inada's book by the title, "Legends from Camp." *Legend,* according to the Webster's Dictionary, is "a nonhistorical or unverifiable story handed down by tradition from earlier times and popularly accepted as historical." To call a lived experience "legend" is to call attention to the problematic way in which we tend to know history as something remote, out there, distanced from us. The dissatisfaction with documentary history has led to an ironic stance held by the poet as historian, who works against the grain of standardized or neutralized verifiability and would rather label his own lived experience, in a tongue-in-cheek fashion, "legends."

But these are indeed legends if we understand the word by its etymology: *legend* comes from medieval English and French "legende," "legere," meaning "to gather, select, read," and it is also akin to Greek "legein": "to gather, say; logos, speech, word, reason." In this sense the poet/historian works as a collector of folktales, of stories "handed down by tradition," and organizes them into a collection to which he assigns a title both ironic and truthful. If the internment camp is a collection of human beings who have been stripped of their own individualities and

INSTRUCTIONS
TO ALL PERSONS OF
JAPANESE
ANCESTRY
Living in the Following Area:

All of that portion of the City of Los Angeles, State of California, within that boundary beginning at the point at which North Figueroa Street meets a line following the middle of the Los Angeles River; thence southerly and following the said line to East First Street; thence westerly on East First Street to Alameda Street; thence southerly on Alameda Street to East Third Street; thence northwesterly on East Third Street to Main Street; thence northerly on Main Street to First Street; thence north-westerly on First Street to Figueroa Street; thence northeasterly on Figueroa Street to the point of beginning.

Pursuant to the provisions of Civilian Exclusion Order No. 33, this Headquarters, dated May 3, 1942, all persons of Japanese ancestry, both alien and non-alien, will be evacuated from the above area by 12 o'clock noon, P. W. T., Saturday, May 9, 1942.

No Japanese person living in the above area will be permitted to change residence after 12 o'clock noon, P. W. T., Sunday, May 3, 1942, without obtaining special permission from the representative of the Commanding General, Southern California Sector, at the Civil Control Station located at:

Japanese Union Church,
120 North San Pedro Street,
Los Angeles, California.

Such permits will only be granted for the purpose of uniting members of a family, or in cases of grave emergency.

The Civil Control Station is equipped to assist the Japanese population affected by this evacuation in the following ways:

1. Give advice and instructions on the evacuation.
2. Provide services with respect to the management, leasing, sale, storage or other disposition of most kinds of property, such as real estate, business and professional equipment, household goods, boats, automobiles and livestock.
3. Provide temporary residence elsewhere for all Japanese in family groups.
4. Transport persons and a limited amount of clothing and equipment to their new residence.

The Following Instructions Must Be Observed:

1. A responsible member of each family, preferably the head of the family, or the person in whose name most of the property is held, and each individual living alone, will report to the Civil Control Station to receive further instructions. This must be done between 8:00 A. M. and 5:00 P. M. on Monday, May 4, 1942, or between 8:00 A. M. and 5:00 P. M. on Tuesday, May 5, 1942.
2. Evacuees must carry with them on departure for the Assembly Center, the following property:
   (a) Bedding and linens (no mattress) for each member of the family;
   (b) Toilet articles for each member of the family;
   (c) Extra clothing for each member of the family;
   (d) Sufficient knives, forks, spoons, plates, bowls and cups for each member of the family;
   (e) Essential personal effects for each member of the family.

All items carried will be securely packaged, tied and plainly marked with the name of the owner and numbered in accordance with instructions obtained at the Civil Control Station. The size and number of packages is limited to that which can be carried by the individual or family group.

3. No pets of any kind will be permitted.
4. No personal items and no household goods will be shipped to the Assembly Center.
5. The United States Government through its agencies will provide for the storage, at the sole risk of the owner, of the more substantial household items, such as iceboxes, washing machines, pianos and other heavy furniture. Cooking utensils and other small items will be accepted for storage if crated, packed and plainly marked with the name and address of the owner. Only one name and address will be used by a given family.
6. Each family, and individual living alone, will be furnished transportation to the Assembly Center or will be authorized to travel by private automobile in a supervised group. All instructions pertaining to the movement will be obtained at the Civil Control Station.

Go to the Civil Control Station between the hours of 8:00 A.M. and 5:00 P.M., Monday, May 4, 1942, or between the hours of 8:00 A.M. and 5:00 P.M., Tuesday, May 5, 1942, to receive further instructions.

J. L. DeWITT
Lieutenant General, U. S. Army
Commanding

SEE CIVILIAN EXCLUSION ORDER NO. 33.

Instructions to All Persons

Let us take
what we can
for the occasion:

> Ancestry. *(Ancestry)*
> All of that portion. *(Portion)*
> With the boundary. *(Boundary)*
> Beginning. *(Beginning)*
> At the point. *(Point)*
> Meets a line. *(Line)*
> Following the middle. *(Middle)*
> Thence southerly. *(Southerly)*
> Following the said line. *(Following) (Said)*
> Thence westerly. *(Westerly)*
> Thence northerly. *(Northerly)*
> To the point. *(Point)*
> Of beginning. *(Beginning) (Ancestry)*

Let us bring
what we need
for the meeting:

> Provisions. *(Provisions)*
> Permission. *(Permission)*
> Commanding. *(Commanding)*
> Uniting. *(Uniting)*
> Family. *(Family)*

Let us have
what we have
for the gathering:

> Civil. *(Civil)*
> Ways. *(Ways)*
> Services. *(Services)*

Figure 10.2   *Legends from Camp*, pp. 4–5.

assigned the same label, this collection of legends, which, as we see, tell stories about individual internees, embodies both the principle of collection and its undoing. It is a camp set up against another camp. But to build such a camp, the poet needs materials; and these are the "matters," which Inada has said, he has taken "into my own hands" (*Legends* 3). They include the linguistic matters that the poet has taken out of the official historical document, which opens the poetic sequence (see Fig. 10.2).

The reproduced document, the infamous Executive Order from Commander J. L. DeWitt, which resulted in the dislocation of over 120,000 Japanese Americans to 10 internment camps in 7 states from 1942 to 1946, should be regarded as a "found" object or concrete poem. As in a modernist work, the large typeface for the ethnic label "JAPANESE" contrasts with the fine print of legal minutiae. If in official history and its authorized revision such a document is often installed as an imposing monument, the poet feels, however, "there's more to life than that." He needs to take the monument apart, taking its bits and pieces, words and phrases, creating his own "order":

> Let us take
> what we can
> for the occasion:
>
>> Ancestry. (*Ancestry*)
>> All of that portion. (*Portion*)
>> With the boundary. (*Boundary*)
>> Beginning. (*Beginning*)
>> At the point. (*Point*)
>> Meets a line. (*Line*)
>> Following the middle. (*Middle*)
>> Thence southerly. (*Southerly*)
>> Following the said line. (*Following*) (*Said*)
>> Thence westerly. (*Westerly*)
>> Thence northerly. (*Northerly*)
>> To the point. (*Point*)
>> Of beginning. (*Beginning*) (*Ancestry*) (5)

Except for the imperative statement starting with "Let us take," what "we" actually "take" are all words and phrases from the Executive Order. But the quotes are further quoted, italicized, and parenthesized: "Ancestry. (*Ancestry*) / All of that portion. (*Portion*)." There are tensions between the poet's desire to generalize and his attempt to particularize the camp experience. On the one hand, the quote and requote, taking words further and further out of their context, resonate with the poet's statement in the introduction: "What did I find? What I *expected* to find: Aspects of humanity, the human condition" (3). The camp experience, the poet seems to insist, is not just Japanese Americans' experience, but also the human experience; their suffering is also human suffering. Hence, the title of the Executive Order, "Instructions to All Persons of Japanese Ancestry," is changed into "Instructions to All Persons" and becomes the title of Inada's poem.

On the other hand, the quote and requote, italicization, and parenthesization are also traces of the poet's personal involvement in otherwise generalized, objectified history. Both the italicization and parenthesization are framing devices that mark each word as irrevocably his own. Parentheses, like the walls and barbed wires of a concentration camp, delineate an enclosed space in which displaced words dwell under the poet's personal care and the reader's private watch. In the context of the poetic sequence's emphasis on childhood motifs—the photo of the boy that opens the sequence, his fantasy of President Roosevelt calling young Lawson Inada, and the large percentage of poems devoted to children in the camp—we may say that such efforts of personalization by claiming words/objects as his own can be related to D. W. Winnicott's famous concepts of "transitional objects" and "transitional phenomena."

According to Winnicott, a newborn baby is not able to distinguish between herself and the world out there, between "me" and "not me." When her brain grows further, she slowly recognizes the difference between external reality and inner self. This is a moment of radical differentiation, a potentially alienating and traumatic experience for the child. But between her inability and her growing ability to recognize and accept reality, Winnicott proposes the existence of an intermediate state that provides a cushion for the transition. The comfort of a (smelly) blanket, the familiarity of a teddy bear, a pillow, and the like all constitute transitional objects that help to alleviate the "strain of relating inner and outer reality." "This intermediate area of experience," Winnicott concludes, "unchallenged in respect to its belonging to inner or external (shared) reality, constitutes the greater part of the infant's experience, and throughout life is retained in the intense experiencing that belongs to the arts and to religion and to imaginative living, and to creative scientific work."[6]

Considering the kind of horror Winnicott has ascribed to the intense alienation of the child from the world ("not-me"), the kind of "remoteness" Inada has attributed to history may indeed be a symptom of difficult psychological transitions. By clinging to words/objects as his own and inventing his own legends as opposed to relying on objective history, the poet is in a sense trying to hold onto those transitional objects, objects that he can identify as part of himself. For a group of people ("persons of Japanese Ancestry") who have become extremely vulnerable to outside violence as a result of displacement, transitional objects are also needed to help them go through this painful process of transition; hence, "Let us take / what we can / for the occasion," as the poet suggests, taking the words and phrases out of an alienating document and putting them into our own hands.

A monument, built to commemorate the historical past, can be equally alienating because of its artificiality and officiality. Tall and massive monuments, such as the Washington Monument and the Lincoln Memorials, impose a sense of history on viewers with the assistance of official historical narrative. To Inada, such monuments would be just as dissatisfying as the Executive Order, which is figuratively a monument in history books, for the purpose of "knowing" history. To counteract such monumental effects of official history, Inada resorts to a poetic strategy of lyricizing the ordinary, such as in this poem, entitled "The Legend of the Jerome Smokestack":

> There is no legend.
> It just stands there
> in a grassy field,
> the brush of swampland,
> soaring up to the sky.
>
> It's just the tallest
> thing around for miles.
> Pilots fly by it.
>
> Some might say it's
> a tribute, a monument,
> a memorial to something.
> But no, not really.
>
> It's just a massive
> stack of skills, labor,

a multitude of bricks.
And what it expressed
was exhaust, and waste.

It's just a pile of past.
Home of the wind, rain,
residence of bodies, nests.
I suppose it even sings.

But no, it's not legend.
It just stands, withstands. (*Legends* 16–17)

In this poem, the Jerome Smokestack refers to the deserted smokestack that can be seen from the internment camp in Jerome, Arkansas (see Fig. 10.3). The "tallest/thing around for miles," the smokestack was a witness to the internees' daily lives. Therefore, "Some might say it's/a tribute, a monument,/a memorial to something." But the poet denies emphatically

Figure 10.3 "Jerome Smokestack." Used by permission of the artist, Joan Myers.

and repeatedly the smokestack's monumental status: "But no, not really," "There is no legend," and "But no, it's not legend." His persistent use of the word "just," as in "It just stands there," "It's just the tallest," "It's just a massive," "It's just a pile of past," and "It just stands, withstands," seems a poetic attempt to do *justice* to the experience, to prevent the kind of alienation induced by monumental history, which tends to make the past larger than life but also rigid, "remote," unsatisfactory.

In "On the Uses and Disadvantages of History for Life," Friedrich Nietzsche draws distinctions among three kinds of history: monumental history, antiquarian history, and critical history. He attacks monumental history for its uncritical nature and for its service only to power. "That the great moments in the struggle of the human individual constitute a chain, that this chain unites mankind across the millennia like a range of human mountain peaks, that the summit of such a long-ago moment shall be for me still living, bright and great—that is the fundamental idea of the faith in humanity which finds expression in the demand for a monumental history." The analogical structure that buttresses such a historical idea, Nietzsche charges, is deceitful, because "how inexact, fluid and provisional that comparison would be! How much of the past would have to be overlooked if it was to produce that mighty effect, how violently what is individual in it would have to be forced into a universal mould and all its sharp corners and hard outlines broken up in the interest of conformity!"[7]

Interestingly, Nietzsche also attacks antiquarian history for its obsession with the past for the sake of the past: "The trivial, circumscribed, decaying and obsolete acquire their own dignity and inviolability through the fact that the preserving and revering soul of the antiquarian man has emigrated into them and there made its home. The history of city becomes for him the history of himself; he reads its walls, its towered gate, its rules and regulations, its holidays, like an illuminated diary of his youth and in all this he finds again himself, his force, his industry, his joy, his judgment, his folly and his vices."[8] The folly and vice of such a use of history lie in that "antiquarian history itself degenerates from the moment it is no longer animated and inspired by the fresh life of the present" and that the antiquarian historian "sinks so low that in the end he is content to gobble down any food whatever, even the dust of bibliographical minutiae."[9]

Walter Benjamin, however, attempts to resuscitate the critical aspects of antiquarian history, claiming that antiquarianism forestalls the long march of teleological history, that an antiquarian collector is anarchistic, destructive, and subversive in a society that prefers exchange, abstraction, and progress to use, singularity, and stasis. (See Part Two in this book for more discussion of Benjamin's reconceptualization of antiquarianism.) Partly in response to Nietzsche's demand that we use history critically, use it in service to the life of the present, Benjamin proposes that some historical truth is buried in the kind of decadence and decay cherished by antiquaries. Speaking about German tragic drama (*Trauerspiel*), Benjamin writes, "That which lies here in ruins, the highly significant fragment, the remnant, is, in fact, the finest material in baroque creation. For it is common practice in the literature of the baroque to pile up fragments ceaselessly, without any strict idea of a goal, and, in the unremitting expectation of a miracle, to take the repetition of stereotypes for a process of intensification."[10]

My detour via Nietzsche and Benjamin is meant not only to reinforce my interpretation of Inada's critique of monumental history, but more importantly, to provide a background for my reading of the Jerome Smokestack poem, in which the poet seeks to occupy an almost antiquarianist position by denying the smokestack the possibility of being monumentalized, by insisting on its *justness*, its being "just a pile of past." Read in this way, the poem pertains to the issues of collection discussed earlier in this book. Better still, by portraying the smokestack as an expression of "exhaust" and "waste," "home of the wind, rain,/residence of bodies, nests," the poem comes tantalizingly close to Benjamin's idea of natural history expressed in his study of *Trauerspiel*: "When, as is the case in the Trauerspiel, history becomes part of the setting, it does so as script. The word 'history' stands written on the countenance of nature in the characters of transience. The allegorical physiognomy of the nature-history, which is put on stage in the Trauerspiel, is present in reality in the form of the ruin. In the ruin history has physically merged into the setting. And in this guise history does not assume the form of process of an eternal life so much as that of irresistible decay."[11] Whereas denying the smokestack's status as a memorial is an outright rejection of monumental history, recognizing its "standing" and "withstanding" among natural ruins is an even more radical critique of the inability of official history to do justice to the justness of the multitudinous details of camp experience, an experience that the poet has tried to revisit, not by means of romanticization, but by means of intentional trivialization.

One symptom of such intentional trivialization is that, despite the awe-provoking word "legend," most legends in Inada's poetic sequence contain nothing legendary at all, as in this poem, entitled "The Legend of the Great Escape":

> The people were passive:
> Even when a train paused
> in the Great Plains, even
> when soldiers were eating,
> they didn't try to escape. (*Legends* 12)

The title of the poem promises a legendary event of the "Great Escape." But the poem itself alludes, anticlimactically, to what did not take place; and rather than portray legendary heroism of "the people," it admits that they were "passive." The intentional flatness of this poem may be surpassed only by the following one-liner, entitled "The Legend of Buddha":

> Buddha said we were all buddhas. (24)

It may be an indirect quote from a Buddhist text; or, more likely, Buddha is a name of an internee, which would make the whole poem, again, a quoted indirect speech. Either way, our critical desire to go deeper into the interior of the poem is met with resistance from the flatness of the line, resonating perhaps with the poet's repeated claim in another poem, "The Legend of Other Camps,"

> It was tough enough deciphering
> what was going on right there.

And,

> It was tough enough deciphering
> what was going on anywhere. (21)

The internees' inability to decipher their environment, coupled with the lackluster events of their ordinary life as portrayed by the poet, illustrates their helplessness in the state of displacement.

But such an inability to decipher is also attributable to the reader of Inada's poetry. Earlier in this book, I discuss the implications of antiquarian collection as a poetic attempt to reject hermeneutical penetration and containment. In *Legends from Camp*, the poet pulls together words, names, and other found objects and creates a collection of legends that are not legendary at all but rather resist our desire to transcend them. As the poet reminds us in the Prologue to the sequence,

> "Among others"—that is important also. Therefore, let's not forget contractors, carpenters, plumbers, electricians and architects, sewage engineers, and all the untold thousands who provided the materials, decisions, energy, and transportation to make the camps a success, including, of course, the administrators, clerks, and families who not only swelled the population but were there to make and keep things shipshape according to D.C. directives and people deploying coffee in the various offices of the WRA, overlooking rivers, cityscapes, bays, whereas in actual camp the troops—excluding, of course, our aunts and uncles and sisters and brothers and fathers and mothers serving stateside, in the South Pacific, the European theater—pretty much had things in order; finally, there were the grandparents, who since the turn of the century, simply assumed they were living in America "among others." (7–8)

The camp is a collection of people, an arrangement that makes them easy to distinguish and decipher (and possibly, destroy). Inada follows the ill-logic of camp collection, foregrounding the arrangedness of the camp by reproducing in his own poems, not decipherable events, but words and phrases, making his poems self-consciously an assemblage.

"The writer," Benjamin warns, "must not conceal the fact that his activity is one of arranging, since it was not so much the mere whole as its obviously constructed quality that was the principal impression which was aimed at."[12] As exemplified by the Executive Order of removal, the state as the author of spatial arrangement of citizens adopts an abstract, legal language to disguise the "constructed quality" of camps and neutralize the violence and impact of the dislocation. To counteract such a remote sense of history, Inada alerts the reader to the existence of "real" people involved in the construction of camps and thereby personalizes the experience. There was once a Jewish woman who had survived the Holocaust. After World War II, whenever she was asked how many children she had, she would refuse to answer the question directly with a number, but say instead, "I have a daughter named Maya, a son Isaac, and another daughter Rachel . . ." By naming her children individually rather than count them as a group/number like members of a camp, she shuns the destructive logic of abstraction of the Holocaust.

"A whole history remains to be written of spaces," Michel Foucault once said, "which would at the same time be the history of powers . . .

from the great strategies of geo-politics to the little tactics of the habitat."[13] The dislocation of Japanese Americans is an instance of such "great strategies of geo-politics" adopted by the imperial state power, a production of abstract space that, according to Henri Lefebvre, functions like a plane, bulldozer, or tank, grinding down and crushing everything before them.[14] In contrast, Inada's attempt to redraw the space of the camps through textual re-placement may represent Foucault's "little tactics of the habitat." Atlanta is indeed "their problem" and the Pacific, as is, is too big a problem. Therefore, we need to shrink the ocean and personalize the history. In Inada's words, we need personalized "legends" to counter the chilling effects of the remoteness of history.

11

Mapping Histories:
Theresa Hak Kyung Cha

The irony is deep in the graffito that opens Theresa Hak Kyung Cha's *Dictee:* a poorly reproduced photo of a graffito that was supposedly created by Korean laborers forced by the Japanese to build underground tunnels during World War II. The blurred quality of the reproduction, the vertical scrawling of Korean words, the solidly dark background splashed with white blotches—all these combine to produce an almost impenetrable entrance to the book (see Fig. 11.1).[1]

Ironically, however, not only is the provenance of the graffito uncertain, but its authenticity has also been called into question. According to Laura Hyun Yi Kang, there is some speculation concerning the "authenticity" of this inscription. The message is inscribed in a tunnel in Nagano Prefecture, Matsushiro City. During the war, imported Korean laborers were employed in constructing a new palace for Japan's emperor to provide an alternative site away from Tokyo. However, the written style of this inscription follows the grammatical rules of Han-gul that were instituted by Korean linguists and scholars after Korea's liberation from Japanese rule. This has led some to believe that the message was written after the liberation.[2]

Use of an object of such a dubious provenance as evidence to a history of utter horror may indeed characterize the remarkably baffling poetics of history that *Dictee* has enacted. Instances of intentional "false documentation" are legion in this book: A quote from Sappho is not part of the works that are generally assumed to be authored by Sappho; Cha names "Elitere" as the muse of lyric poetry instead of Euterpe; and Sam Choy, the Honolulu chef, appears in a list of elements representing

Figure 11.1 Theresa Cha, *Dictee*, frontispiece.

"Heaven, Earth, and Humans."[3] As a book that is preoccupied with history and historiography, *Dictee* reveals over and over again the "deadly space between" fiction and documentation—deadly because both genres, with their deceiving and self-deceiving claims to discursive coherence and textual stability, often disallow any crossover, transgression, or any view that is from neither outside nor inside. The Korean graffito—and in a sense the whole book of *Dictee*—occupies such a deadly space, a stain (and stained) glass, telling a history of horror from a precarious, almost unsustainable discursive position. Following the nearly vertical lines of the Korean sentences, from right to left ("Mother, I miss you"), to the middle ("I'm hungry"), and then from left to right ("I want to go home"), readers are caught in a circular reading, with no view of the outside or the road to the inside: "Opaque. Reflects/never" (126). This is a scene of reading that Juliana Spahr, commenting on *Dictee*, has characterized as "decolonizing reading" and that Mary Ann Caws, in a different context, would call "stressful reading."

According to Spahr, *Dictee* is "built around discomfort. It has little reading ease. It often teases and encourages readers to question what they take as proper, correct, or true. It gives false information, both obvious and not so obvious, along with verifiable facts." Adopting such radical compositional principles, Cha pursues not simply a critique of colonization on the level of content, but also an effect of decolonizing reading. If conventional reading, as a learned and regulated act, is predicated on the reader's ability and desire to read for mastery, development, identification, or conclusion, *Dictee* challenges these abilities and frustrates these desires by seeking to undo readings that result in either the reader's colonization of the text or her conquest by the text. As opposed to the hermeneutic/colonialist model of reading, Cha invites the reader to enter "into a creative and self-reflexive relation" with the text, a relation in which "both readers and works matter."[4]

To Caws, such a reader/text relation or involvement leads to a reading situation that she calls "stressful." By "stress," she means first "in the sense of a certain anxiety relating to the projects both of comparison and of expression of that comparison: to relate occasions stress. Secondly, as in metric stress, it is an accent placed on certain details in particular, sometimes in a recurring pattern. Lastly, there is the stress of a 'stressed' metal, where the trying moment proves some sort of endurance."[5] What Spahr and Caws have described are problematics of reading that cannot simply be resolved by hermeneutic means. To read *Dictee*, as Naoki Sakai reminds us, "requires a different kind of labor,"[6] just as Cha suggests that to know history means to implicate ourselves in *that* history:

> To the other nations who are not witnesses, who are not subject to the same oppressions, they cannot know. Unfathomable the words, the terminology: enemy, atrocities, conquest, betrayal, invasion, destruction. They exist only in the larger perception of History's recording, that affirmed, admittedly and unmistakably, one enemy nation has disregarded the humanity of another. Not physical enough. Not to the very flesh and bone, to the core, to the mark, to the point where it is necessary to intervene, even if to invent anew, expressions, for *this* experience, for this *outcome,* that does not cease to continue.
>
> To the others, these accounts are about (one more) distant land, like (any other) distant land, without any discernable features in the narrative, (all the same) distant like any other.
>
> This document is transmitted through, by the same means, the same channel without distinction the content is delivered in the same style: the word. The image. To appeal to the masses to congeal the information

to make bland, mundane, no longer able to transcend their own conspirator method, no matter how alluring their presentation. The response is
precoded to perform predictably however passively possible. Neutralized
to achieve the no-response, to make absorb, to submit to the unidirectional correspondance [sic]. (32–33)

In this often-quoted passage, Cha appears to refer to the history of
Japan's annexation and colonial rule of Korea: "On August 29, 1910,
[the Korean Emperor] Sunjong was forced to issue a proclamation
yielding up both his throne and his country. Thus the Korean nation,
against the will of its entire people, was handed over to the harsh colonial rule of Japan by a coterie of traitors." Ki-baik Lee, in his highly regarded book of Korean history, goes on to say, "In its preamble, the
treaty declared that Japan's annexation of Korea was intended to 'pro-
mote the common wealth of the two nations and to assure permanent
peace' in Asia. Japan, however, was not a friend of Korea but its enemy.
Japan had annexed Korea to enhance the prosperity of the Japanese
people at the expense of the people of Korea."[7] This history deeply complicates the picture of the transpacific: It is no longer a paradigm of the
East versus the West, Japan versus America, or China versus America.
The internal colonization within the East Asian region renders any
geopolitical dichotomy close to moot.

For Cha, however, the problem does not lie solely in the dichotomy;
she questions history itself as a body of archived and retrievable knowledge. If history, like Lee's book, functions only as "recording," "document," or "information," then the readers "who are not witnesses, who are
not subject to the same oppressions," Cha emphatically claims, "cannot
know." For a reader to go through a normative and normalizing reading
process in which historical knowledge has been "neutralized," made
"bland, mundane," it actually makes the reader into a "conspirator" of
the oppressor. The task of inventing an alternative to conventional history that Cha has set up for herself would be to write a history that is
"physical enough," "to the very flesh and bone, to the core, to the mark,
to the point where it is necessary to intervene." To achieve such an in-
terventionist goal, the book needs to be written and read in a radically
unconsumable way.

In appearance, Dictee is constructed almost like an archive, but as
Anne Anlin Cheng has pointed out, it is an archive with "antidocumen-
tary desires." Unlike material in a conventional archive or museum, in

Dictee "evidences . . . are conspicuously lacking in proper documentation. None of the images are captioned or footnoted; the same may be said of the clearly plagiarized citations."[8] One uncaptioned image is this photograph of execution (see Fig. 11.2): three blindfolded figures in traditional Korean clothes, with arms extended outward, facing a team of executioners who may be identified by their military uniforms as Korean collaborators of Japan ("a coterie of traitors" in Lee's book).

Writing about photography, Susan Sontag argues that atrocity photographs of the sort that might move people to transnational action do not produce real or genuine experience. They produce only a dangerous semblance of experience, a tourist's detached voyeurism: "Essentially

Figure 11.2 *Dictee,* p. 39.

the camera makes everyone a tourist in other people's reality, and eventually in one's own."[9] Commenting on the "scandalous deficiency" of postwar German representations of the destruction of cities by the Allied Forces at the end of World War II, W. G. Sebald tells us that "to this day, any concern with the real scenes of horror during the catastrophe still has an aura of the forbidden about it, even of voyeurism, something that these notes of mine have not entirely been able to avoid. I was not surprised when a teacher in Detmold told me, a little while ago, that as a boy in the immediate postwar years he quite often saw photographs of the corpses lying in the streets after the firestorm brought out from under the counter of a Hamburg secondhand bookshop, to be fingered and examined in a way usually reserved for pornography."[10] Does the execution photo in *Dictee* fall into the same voyeuristic trap?

In *Dictee*, in a section immediately preceding the photo, one comes across passages that read:

> Some will not know age. Some not age. Time stops. Time will stop for some. For them especially. Eternal time. No age. Time fixes for some. Their image, the memory of them is not given to deterioration, unlike the captured image that extracts from the soul precisely by reproducing, multiplying itself. Their countenance evokes not the hallowed beauty, beauty from seasonal decay, evokes not the inevitable, not death, but the dy-ing.
>
> Face to face with memory, it misses. It's missing. Still. What of time. Does not move. Remains there. Misses nothing. Time, that is. All else. All things else. All other, subject to time. Must answer to time, except. Still born. Aborted. Barely. Infant. Seed, germ, sprout, less even. Dormant. Stagnant. Missing. (37–38)

And immediately after the photo comes this image of a handwritten, manuscript page (see Fig. 11.3). In terms of content, the manuscript page appears to be the "origin" of the printed passages that one has come across before the scene of execution. Noticing the simulacrum, a curious reader may turn the pages back and compare the printed passages with the manuscript. In the process of turning the pages back and forth—a readerly practice *Dictee* has obviously invited—the reader will inevitably re-witness again and again the scene of execution. Given Cha's penchant for frustrating hermeneutical desires, desires that would turn readers into unwilling "conspirators" of historical atrocities by virtue of their precoded unidirectional response, the photo of execution seems to have been planted there and demands the reader's repeated visit as a result of the correspondence between the printed and manuscript pages. Rather than a simple object for voyeuristic viewing, this image guides the reader into contact with history not as a knower ("they cannot know"), but as a witness in a carefully structured text that foregrounds its own structure. As Derrida says, "what is no longer archived in the same way is no longer lived in the same way. Archivable meaning is also and in advance codetermined by the structure that archives."[11] Or, as Cha once quoted Jean-Luc Godard's reply to the question "You have repeatedly defined the difference between making a political film

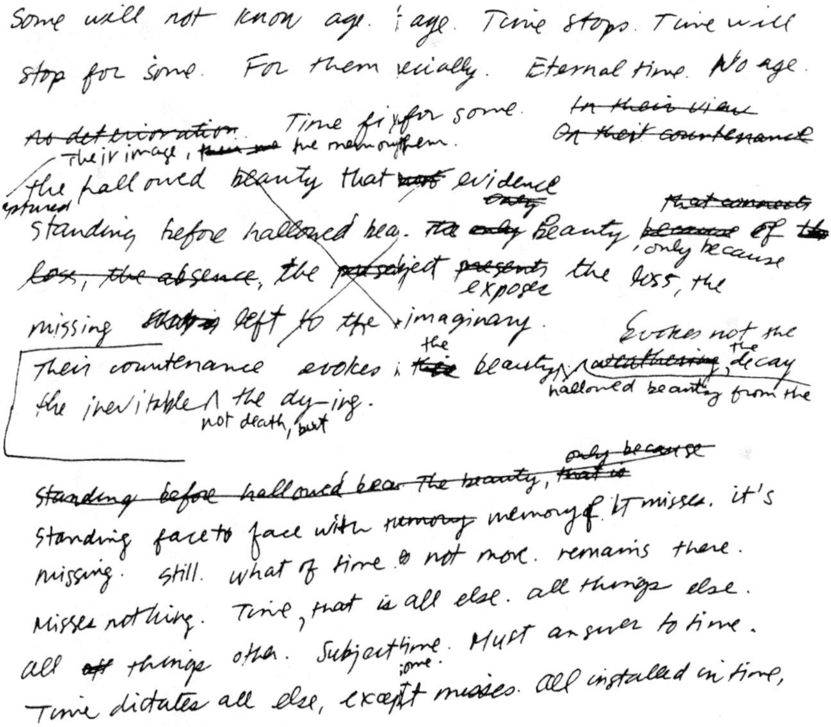

Figure 11.3 *Dictee*, pp. 40–41.

and making a film politically": "Yes, these two things are completely different. As Brecht already said, it's not important to know what are the real things but rather how things are real. The relation is in the reality." Cha insists that we study the apparatus or medium of representation rather than "conceal from its spectator the relationship of the viewer/subject to the work being viewed."[12]

By inducing the reader to turn pages back and forth, Cha not only creates a montage effect for the texts and images, but also destabilizes printed words—a chosen instrument for official, documentary history. The lack of faithful correspondence between the printed passages and the manuscript note, as we see above, produces a quality of tentativeness for both textual apparatuses. In Figures 11.4 and 11.5, Cha once again applies her skills as an experimental filmmaker and plays on the effects of visual contrasts. Figure 11.4 is a side view of air passages and lungs of a human being, and Figure 11.5 is a map of the Korean Peninsula.

The striking visual resemblance between the two images (the protruding chin, concaving back of the neck, and the shape of the lungs all find eerie resemblances in the map) speaks volumes about colonial violence.[13] We notice that in the anatomy of vocal organs, words such as "nasal passage," "pharynx," "larynx," and "esophagus" are merely scientific terms for those parts of a human body; they are not words that actually come out of the body. In other words, the body is silent or silenced because the vocal organs have become merely objects for anatomical study:

> No organ. Anymore.
> Cries.
>
> . . .
>
> Phrases   silent
> Paragraphs   silent
> Pages and pages a little nearer
> to movement
> line
> after line
> void to the left to the right.
> Void the words.
> Void the silence. (73)

Like the human body in Figure 11.4, the Korean Peninsula in Figure 11.5 is also subject to descriptive violence and is unable to speak for itself. All

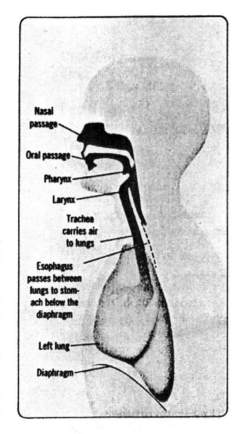

Figure 11.4 *Dictee*, p. 74.

Figure 11.5 *Dictee*, p. 78.

the words on the map are in English rather than Korean, and most striking of all is the name to the right: "Sea Of Japan." As J. Hillis Miller reminds us, topography contains "the politics of nationalism as they involve border demarcations and territorial appropriations. Deciding whether to have street signs in French in Montreal or in Welsh in Wales is not a trivial issue."[14] Miller understands topography as essentially a speech act by virtue of its ability to name and rename, mark and remark. The part of the Pacific that is called the "Sea of Japan" on Cha's map is also called the "East Sea."[15] The appropriative and counterappropriative desires of topographical naming need no illustration here. But when Cha adopts in her text an English map imagined from colonizing Japan's perspective and contrasts it with a map of anatomized human vocal organs, the name "Sea of Japan" reveals at once its colonial power and its fictionality as printed words.[16] It is as if the whole peninsula had been silenced by the words that are alien to native topographical imagination. Is this why *Dictee,* as some have pointed out, almost never uses Korean words? Because the curious absence is actually a poetic, albeit silent, protest against the violence of colonial naming?

It is in this name of "Sea of Japan" that Cha's reader-as-conspirator thesis becomes most striking. Just as we study the anatomy of a dead body that cannot speak back to us, our reading of a map and consequent acquisition or renewal of topographical knowledge will undoubtedly make us conspirators in the colonial history, UNLESS we learn to read differently. If we "cannot know" because we did not "witness" the events in the past, then we can at least stand witness to the textual violence that always accompanies other kinds of violence. To be able to hear the silenced words, to see what is not there, to read words not as *dictated* to us from the book, is indeed a process of decolonizing reading, which may be stressful for an otherwise passive reader but utterly needs to be stressed.

Dictee, if we learn to read differently and not as dictated, is an anagram of deceit. And Cha reminds us:

> One is deceived. One was deceived of the view
> outside inside stain glass. Opaque. Reflects
> never. (126)

As Derrida says, "The question of the archive is not . . . a question of the past. It is not the question of a concept dealing with the past that might already be at our disposal or not at our disposal, an archivable concept of the archive. It is a question of the future, the question of the future itself, the question of a response, of a promise and of a responsibility for tomorrow."[17] The "never" that is "reflected" in *Dictee* is such a tomorrow we as readers of history will have to bear witness to.

Conclusion:
Between History and Literature—
A Poetics of Acknowledgment

The apparition   of these faces   in the crowd   :
Petals   on a wet, black   bough   .

—Ezra Pound, "In a Station of the Metro" (1913)

In the history of transpacific imagination, nothing may sound as outrageous as T. S. Eliot's assertion that Ezra Pound was "the inventor of Chinese poetry." Seen in a different light, however, Eliot may be right: He does qualify his term by calling Pound the inventor of Chinese poetry "for our time"; that is, Pound did not invent Chinese poetry as such but Chinese poetry in English translation.[1] In my previous book, *Transpacific Displacement* (2002), I study the complexity of translation in such contexts and suggest that a seemingly simple poem, such as "In a Station of the Metro," contains a long history of dislocation and transformation of cultural meanings across the Pacific. My current book continues the theme of the transpacific but with a different focus. If in *Transpacific Displacement* I am mostly concerned with the poetic field of textual migration saturated with cross-cultural ideology, in this book I am interested in the ways in which literature and history at times underpin and at others undermine each other's work. In other words, this book describes the precarious crossover of these two regimes of discourse in the geopolitics of transpacific imagination.

We are all familiar with Hegel's infamous formulation of the History of the World traveling from the East to the West, "for Europe is absolutely the end of History, Asia the beginning." Using a poetic metaphor, Hegel proclaims that in the East rises the outward physical Sun and in the West it sinks down but "here consentaneously rises the Sun of self-consciousness, which diffuses a nobler brilliance."[2] As it turns out, the German word for the East or Orient is *das Morgenland,* literally meaning "the morning land"; and the German word for the West or Occident is *das Abendland,* literally "the evening land." Could it be, we want to ask, that Hegel was tricked by his native tongue? Could it be that Hegel's philosophical historiography is yet another example of ethnocentrism fostered by language? To make such a claim without reservation is to exaggerate the power of poetic language and to ignore both the depth of Hegelian philosophy and the empirical facts of world history that seem to support Hegel's formulation: The West has been the dominant force in the past centuries.[3] But to dismiss such a supposition as completely groundless is to miss the point I have tried to make throughout this book: Poetic imagination is the ghost in the machine of History, an apparition that haunts, to paraphrase Heidegger, the house of Historical Being.

By foregrounding the poetics and counterpoetics in historical imagination, I am not trying to repeat some postmodernist truisms.[4] These claims to the fictionality of history, it seems to me, are too easy a way out of the deadlock. Historical experience, as Roger Chartier reminds us, "is not reducible to discourse."[5] But to return to time-honored empiricism, to insist that history is knowable independent of our structure of knowledge, is not a viable solution either. What I have described in this book as counterpoetics in the transpacific imagination are instances of negotiation with these two extreme positions. It seems that the solution to the dilemma is not to seek a solution, but to live with it, live in the gap.

From the White Whale to the White Male (Rage)

As indicated at the conclusion of Part Two of this book, the imaginary can intrude on the real: Close to where Melville's *Pequod* went down in its doomed pursuit of the White Whale, the United States conducted its first offshore testing of nuclear weapons. What Melville calls "that double-bolted land" or "the impenetrable Japans," later in the twentieth century, witnessed a "doubled flowering" of nuclear horror that destroyed two of its cities.

On August 9, 1997, the fifty-second anniversary of the bombings, Japan's leading newspaper, *Asashi Shimbun,* published a feature story entitled "Atomic Bomb Survivor Poet Araki Yasusada Is a Fake":

An atomic bomb survivor poet has become a controversy in American poetry. Born in Kyoto in 1907, Araki lost his wife and daughters in the Hiroshima bombing and died from cancer in 1972. He never published when he was alive, but his notes were found after his death, and the English translations were published one after another. The controversy was not because of the content, but because he was not a real Japanese poet.

In its July/August 1996 issue, the major U.S. journal *American Poetry Review* featured "Doubled Flowering: From the Notebooks of Araki Yasusada," which includes "Loon and Dome," a poem about his wife and daughters who had died from the Hiroshima bombing. The translation was done by three Japanese: Tosa Motoyuki, Okura Kyojin, and Ojiu Norinaga. Also included in the journal are a brief biography of Araki, his portrait, and footnotes about the Hiroshima Industrial Promotion Hall.

Araki's poems and letters in fourteen notebooks have received high praises in the past three or four years in the U.S. According to his biography, Araki was a member of a well-known poetry group and an acquaintance of other famous poets. If this were true, it would have been a discovery of a great poet. But there were rumors that Araki did not exist. The fact became clear when *American Poetry Review* printed an "apology" in the next issue, stating that there was neither Araki nor the three translators, that the poems had been submitted by Kent Johnson, a professor at a junior college in Illinois. Johnson admitted that Araki was fictional, but he insisted that he did not create it but his college friend did. "My friend Tosa wrote them. His name is also fictional, but I can't tell you his real name or nationality."[6]

I quote this Japanese newspaper article for two reasons. First, it captures the gist of the story, which is by now widely known in American literary and academic circles; second, it gives us a rare view of the Japanese response to the incident. Ever since the outbreak of the scandal in 1996, there have been numerous reviews, journalistic reports, academic papers, and Internet discussions devoted to the Yasusada hoax, with opinions ranging between condemning it as an "essentially criminal act" and praising it as one of the most moving and revealing works of poetry written about the effects of the Bomb.[7] Eliot Weinberger perhaps best summarizes the complexity of the issue: Yasusada is "both the greatest poet of Hiroshima and its most unreliable witness."[8]

Curiously absent in these responses, however, is a concern with how the Japanese would regard this issue. The debate has been largely self-reflective and U.S.-centered, circling around postmodern issues of authorship, reader, or text, while leaving out any serious engagement with Japanese historical experience and its representation. A subsequent article in *Asashi Shimbun*, by Akitoshi Nagahata, identifies exactly this problem: "The arguments over Yasusada in magazines, internet discussions, and so on tend to focus on issues of American literature, but not on the reality of atomic bombs."[9] As Marjorie Perloff points out, the attention to the Yasusada hoax has come at the expense of any genuine interest in Japanese postwar poetry.[10] Or as Gayatri Chakravorty Spivak asks: "Who slips into the place of the 'human' of 'humanism' at the end of the day?"[11]

In the book *Death of a Discipline,* from which I have taken the quote, Spivak cautions against the appropriative poetics, the desire to "transcode," that has characterized Area Studies and Comparative Literature over the past decades. She invites us instead to practice "teleopoesis," that is, "to affect the distant in a *poiesis*—an imaginative making—without guarantees" (31). We should, she urges, prepare ourselves for "a patient and provisional and forever deferred arrival into the performance of the other, in order not to transcode but to draw a response" (13). Sadly, however, as we see in the case of Yasusada, cross-cultural and transhistorical imagination has been dominated either by a modernist fallacy of appropriation (the desire to translate the cultural experience of the other into our own terms) or by a postmodernist denial of history (the notion that all history is fictive or constructive and therefore cannot be known empirically). Spivak's argument may help us imagine an ethical ground between the fallacy of appropriation and denial of history, a ground where the other will not disappear either in our empathetic embrace or in our nonchalance, a ground where historical knowledge is possible even if in a very limited way, and where knowledge is replaced by acknowledgment and cognition by recognition.

The defense of the Yasusada hoax relies mostly on the notions of author function, hyper-authorship, and the unreliability of historical knowledge. Following the Foucaultian idea of the "death of the author," defenders (some of whom are actually the "front men" for the fictional Yasusada) have proposed a theory of hyper-authorship as a critique of the current valorization of racial, ethnic, and sexual identity within our culture:

The hyper-authorship is a necessary step in the development of the theory of difference in the direction of "self-differentiation." I differ from myself in many ways, and authorship is the sphere where I create numerous "selves" different from my own . . .

The theory of difference so far has led to many unsatisfactory results, such as deadening of differences in natural origins, such as predetermined ethnic and sexual identities provoking ideological wars among their representatives. The basic contradiction of postmodern theory is between the emphases on (cultural) difference and (racial, ethnic, and sexual) identity. Why should writing be just an instrument in the assertion of one's identity, belonging to a set of natural determinants, such as race, ethnicity, gender, and sexual orientation? Writing is a challenge to my identity whence the series of hyper-authors proceed, different from the biological author and from one another. Writing should be imaginative erasure and transgression of origins rather than their ideological reinstatement. Writing would be a progression of difference in my relationship with myself—and by the same token my increasing involvement and integration with others.[12]

Kent Johnson, the "prime suspect" in the hoax, follows the same line of reasoning and describes an almost fantastic world of fluid authorial identities: "In this resistance to regimentation the circulation of created, fully-realized hyper-authorships will become a vibrant and branching and authentic utopian space, with schools and collaborations, journals and sub-genres, critical forays and epistolary crossings." Johnson further accuses his detractors of practicing censorship in the name of difference:

> Yasusada is not an "appropriation"; he is a deep and idiosyncratic work of empathy, one which provides, in the words of the critic Joe Lockard, "a radical encounter with the thinness of human distinctions." Naturally, this bothers those who demand that empathy have checkpoints at the borders of the "other's" difference. Sweeping away their policing, Yasusada reveals, through the mirrored-layers of his text, how deeply the otherness of Hiroshima and its victims is inside "us."[13]

A term coined in the English language in 1909 to translate the German word *Einfuhlun,* "empathy" designates the self's capacity for identifying sympathetically with what is other to it. Recognized in antiquity as one of the techniques available to orators, empathy was known to rhetoricians as *ethopoeia*—putting yourself in the place of another, so as to understand and express the other person's feelings more vividly. But in the age of pluralism, empathy has become an ideologically suspect myth of benevolence designed by the powerful to justify their practice of selectively appropriating the cultures of the powerless.[14]

It is not that we should set up "checkpoints at the borders of the 'other's' difference," as Johnson accuses. But Johnson's "work of empathy" actually makes light of the ambiguity of the other's experience by claiming to speak for the other. What if the other is not willing to speak in the first place? Cultural historians have noted a peculiar silence or unwillingness to speak on the part of Hiroshima bombing survivors (or, for that matter, on the part of crime victims in general). Indeed, there are complicated reasons for the Japanese survivors' silence. To a large extent, many Japanese felt that the nuclear bombing was punishment for the atrocities Japanese soldiers had committed in Asia, and therefore regarded it as a national "shame" about which they would rather not speak. As Nagahata, the author of the second *Asashi Shimbun* article mentioned earlier, admits, "It is difficult for us to talk about Hiroshima/Nagasaki, because to do so would always make us question our subjectivity. We are sons and daughters of the people who were bombed, but at the same time of the oppressors. We could blame our fate on the politicians at the time (i.e., militarists) or on the war in the abstract. But I think this is an evasion."[15]

Moreover, the silence also speaks to the unspeakable nature of the horror experienced by the victims. As Lisa Yoneyama has told us in her brilliant study of Hiroshima testimonial practices, the people who are willing to come forward and tell their stories have been received with a great deal of suspicion and ambivalence. In contrast, the survivors' reluctance to speak is often regarded as authentication of their experience.[16] Here we are reminded of the 1959 French film *Hiroshima, Mon Amour* (by Alain Resnais and Marguerite Duras), in which any direct referentiality to Hiroshima is circumvented or even denied. In the film a French actress comes to make a movie in Hiroshima and has a passionate affair with a Japanese man who, like Yasusada, has lost his family in the bombing. At first the Japanese man rejects the French woman's assertion that she "saw everything," that she "saw" the horror through the traces it left behind in museums, hospitals, newsreels, landscapes, and so on. As the film evolves, we realize that she does see the horror, but only through the filter of her own love affair at Nevers with a German soldier during the Occupation, an affair that ended when she witnessed his death on the very day they were to run away together. Her claim to know the horror of the Hiroshima bombing, then, is substantiated only indirectly. Empathy works here not through benevolently putting oneself in the place of the other, but by putting oneself in one's own place. There is no desire or possibility to collapse the difference between the two, but only to recognize each in its own. In contrast, the Yasusada text circumvents all the complications embedded in the cultural practice of testimony and resistance to testimony. In its pursuit of empathy and the "thinness of human distinctions," the Yasusada text goes in a direction opposite to what Cathy Caruth, in her fascinating reading of *Hiroshima, Mon Amour,* has called the "indirect referentiality of history": Given the traumatic nature of history, "events are only historical to the extent that they implicate others."[17] As such, the Yasusada case is less one of empathy than it is one of "nuclear universalism," which Yoneyama defines as "the idea that Hiroshima's disaster ought to be remembered from the transcendent and anonymous position of humanity, and that the remembering of Hiroshima's tragedy should invoke natural and commonly shared human thoughts, sentiments, and moral attitudes not limited by cultural boundaries."[18] To see how such universalism works in Yasusada, a close reading is in order.

In the *Asashi Shimbun* article, there is a Yasusada poem along with his portrait. It is the same poem that *American Poetry Review* featured, only this time it appears in Japanese (translation, original, or back-translation?). In its English "original" the poem runs as follows:

> LOON AND DOME
> *January 1, 1947*
>
> The crying girl sounds like a loon . . .
>
> Why does her mournful sound call to mind the sky
> through the dome of the Industrial Promotion Hall?[i]
>
> You told me there you were pregnant with her
> as we strolled through the plaster chambers
> of the giant Model of the Heart.
>
> I have waited all week, you quietly said,
> to be with you here in this magical place,
> and to tell you something beautiful.
>
> (It was your sentimental heart
> that always made me laugh,
> and this stain on the page is spilt tea.)[ii]
>
> [*Yasusada note in margin*] Insert breast-plate stanza here?

Nomura, the long wake of our daughter
vanishes, ceaselessly, in our union.

i. *The Hiroshima Industrial Promotion Hall, a prominent city landmark because of its win-
dowed dome, was one of the few structures left somewhat recognizable after the bombing. Its skeletal
remains have been preserved to the present as a memorial.*
ii. *In the original, there is, indeed, a stain covering the first half of the poem.*[19]

What is curious here is the use of footnotes. One note addresses the
skeletal remains that exist in reality—the Hiroshima Industrial Promotion Hall—and the other a tea stain on a manuscript page that exists, it
now appears, only in fiction. Both are attempts to construct an origin,
the former being the ground zero of a catastrophe and the latter being
the "zero degree" of writing. The close proximity of the two notes seems
to reveal the Yasusada author's desire to approximate the veracity of the
architectural remains for his own textual forgery.

But the Hiroshima Industrial Promotion Hall has a dubious history as
far as its origin is concerned. According to Yoneyama, the design for the
Peace Memorial Park, of which the Hall is an important part, can be
traced back to a nearly identical ground plan that had been adopted
three years before Japan's surrender as part of a grand imperial vision:
the Commemorative Building Project for the Construction of Greater
East Asia. "The unproblematized transition of Hiroshima's commemorative space from celebrating imperial Japan to honoring the postwar
peaceful nation," Yoneyama writes, "suggests the persistence of prewar
social and cultural elements."[20] Yasusada in effect relies on the veracity
of an unstable and problematic history of origin without being able to
challenge the very notion of origin. As Charles Bernstein observes, "literary fraud does not, in itself, destabilize truth claims or authorship
since in many cases . . . the fraud depends on a highly stable idea of authorship for the deception to work." Yasusada's claim to hyper-authorship
does not amount to a critique of origin but to an erasure of origins that are
not "ours." As such, it lends itself to Bernstein's condemnation of it as a
case of white male rage, the "apotheosis of the poetics of resentment in
the 1990s."[21]

Whether or not a case of white male rage, Yasusada simultaneously
relies on the idea of origin and mocks such an origin. It directly feeds on
the historical trauma of Hiroshima and indirectly suggests the impossibility of historical knowledge. As such, it helps us to recognize that the
modernist fallacy of appropriation and the postmodernist denial of

authenticity are but flip sides of the same coin. Appropriation eliminates differences through emulative permeability, whereas denial does so by fictionalizing the differences. Attacking multiculturalism and identity politics in his interview with Bill Freind, Johnson tries, again and again, to separate writing from the biological writer, history from historical experience. Demanding that no "checkpoints" be set up "at the borders of the 'other's' experience," Johnson dreams of a "thinness of human distinctions" made possible through fictionalization. Here history and literature reach a twilight zone, where the two at once wrestle with and flee from each other. Indeed, if history deals with human experience as a problem of epistemology whereas literature approaches that same experience as an issue of ontology, Yasusada's apparent attempt to walk in this deadly space between them ultimately fails to raise any profound questions because, once it is revealed as a hoax, all the disciplinary and cross-disciplinary issues will disappear immediately. When read as "real" work by a "real" author, it relies on the idea of historical origin and authenticity; when known as a hoax, it becomes merely a fiction. There is no crossover, only "doubled flowering."

In *Death of a Discipline,* Spivak seeks to strike a path through the Death Valley between history and literature, or, as regards her immediate concerns, between Area Studies and Comparative Literature. Between Area Studies' claim to know the other objectively and Comparative Literature's desire to empathize with the other subjectively, Spivak proposes a middle ground from which we can look at the other—from a distance, or teleopoetically—not to transcode, but to read with patience and without any *guarantee.* I emphasize this otherwise ordinary word because of its almost (Gertrude) Steinian repetitions in Spivak's book: "the law of curvature—that one cannot access another directly and with a *guarantee*" (30); "to affect the distant in a *poiesis*—an imaginative making—without *guarantees*" (31); "the literary critic who sees in imagination an instrument for giving in, without *guarantees,* to the teleopoietic gaze of others" (45); and "This is imagining yourself, really letting yourself be imagined (experience that impossibility) without *guarantees,* by and in another culture, perhaps" (52). The notion of a "guarantee" speaks both to the self-assurance of objectivity within Area Studies and the self-confidence of navel-gazing within Comparative Literature. The phrase, "without a guarantee," however, points both to the possibility of knowing (history) and to its uncertainty (literature). Only by acknowledging the ontological status of the other and recognizing the epistemological gap in our knowledge, will we ultimately approach the conditions of collectivity and planetarity that Spivak sees as correctives to appropriation and denial. Between "our literature," which Yasusada pretends not to be but actually is, and "their history," the horror of Hiroshima and Nagasaki, lies the possibility of collective responsibility and planetary imagination.

A Poetics of Acknowledgment

The gap between literature and history also pertains to the distance that divides us from the other. In Pound's imagistic poem, the apparition is not just that of the faces, but what hovers between the two lines that resist a metaphoric collapse: faces (as) petals. By calling it an image rather than a simile, Pound tries to make that gap disappear, if not in space, then at least in time. An image, as Pound defines it, is "that which presents an intellectual and emotional complex in *an instant of time.*"[22] Hard as Pound tries, the image of petals both figures and disfigures the faces.

In his meditations on ethics and the face, Emmanuel Levinas writes, "The face resists possession, resists my power. In its epiphany, in expression, the sensible, still graspable, turns into total resistance to the grasp."[23] To Levinas, the Poundian-style poetic conflation, the imaging of the human face, amounts to violent appropriations. "The relation with the face," he insists, should not be "an object-cognition" (75) but instead "a moral summons" (196). In his pursuit of a mode of being where the other will not disappear into the "ontological imperialism" of the same, Levinas adopts on a face-to-face position, which refuses exterior "viewing" or representation: "The face with which the Other turns to me is not reabsorbed in a representation of the face. To hear his destitution which cries out for justice is not to represent an image to oneself, but is to posit oneself as responsible" (215). What Levinas seeks is a position where ontology does not take precedence over fraternity, nor does knowledge take precedence over discourse.

As I was writing this conclusion, on July 22, 2005, there had just been another round of subway bombings in London the day before. Looking over the Internet, I saw an article from *Times Online* that reads in one paragraph: " 'You see customers' faces, they are not happy faces. There is a lot of fear,' said a station attendant at Euston Station, as he explained to a crowd that the Northern Line was suspended. 'All we're trying to do is get back to normal.'"[24] Since 9/11 the normalcy of daily life has changed for most people, and the "faces in the crowd," of passengers on subways/tubes, have carried expressions beyond Pound's pre–World War I imagination ("In a Station of the Metro" was published in April 1913). A whole century of violence and horror has dramatically redefined the relation between the same and the other—Levinas's meditation on ethics, we should not forget, has much to do with the Holocaust. The precarious situation may be best summarized by George W. Bush in his incendiary speech made immediately after 9/11: "If you are not with us, you are with the terrorists." What caught my attention was the word "with," on which Bush had put a rhetorical spin according to his divisive, pro-violent ideology.

"With," says Jean-Luc Nancy, "is at the heart of Being." Being, to Nancy, is always "Being Singular Plural," because existence can only be grasped in the "paradoxical simultaneity of togetherness." We say "to speak with," "to sleep with," "to go out with," "to live with," and so on—all signs of the *withness,* a relationship in which there is no absolute subject/object dichotomy and neither side disappears completely into the other.[25] By dividing between "with us" and "with the terrorists" and restricting "with" with a conditional "If" clause, Bush has completely destroyed the ontological multiplicity of existence. His manipulation of the discourse of withness only foregrounds what Levinas sees as the perils of rhetoric as ruse and persuasion. "Rhetoric approaches the other," Levinas reminds us, "not to face him, but obliquely" (70). To approach the other from an angle, with an agenda, is "to lose face (to lose the face of the other and always also to lose one's own face)."[26]

Among modern thinkers, Martin Heidegger was perhaps the first to recognize being-with (*Mitsein, Miteinandersein,* and *Mitdasein*) as essential to Being. "Dasein's . . . understanding of Being," Heidegger writes, "already implies the understanding of others."[27] Heidegger's "A Dialogue on Language," in particular, seems to address the issue of cross-cultural understanding. In this semifictional dialogue, Heidegger discusses the nature of language with his Japanese interlocutor, and his inquiry centers on a key question: "What does the Japanese world understand by language? Asked still more cautiously: Do you have in your language a word for what we call language? If not, how do you experience what with us is called language?"[28] A close reading of the dialogue, however, reveals that Heidegger has adroitly turned an East-West dialogue into "one architectonic monologue."[29] It seems that Heidegger is not really trying to think *with* his interlocutor but *for* him. In the "Dialogue," after a long hesitation and perambulation, the two arrive at an answer:

> *Inquirer*: What is the Japanese word for "language"?
> *Japanese*: *(after further hesitation)* It is *"Koto ba."*
> I: And what does that say?
> J: *ba* means leaves, including and especially the leaves of a blossom—petals. Think of cherry blossoms or plum blossoms.
> I: And what does *Koto* say?
> J: This is the question most difficult to answer. But . . . *Koto* always also names that which in the event gives delight, itself, that which uniquely in each unrepeatable moment comes to radiance in the fullness of its grace.
> I: *Koto,* then, would be the appropriating occurrence of the lightening message of grace.
> J: Beautifully said! (45)

This is a classic scene of anthropological fieldwork: An ethnographer asks questions prepared from preconceived notions and waits for the native informant to fill in the blanks. In terms of comparative poetics, this is what Haun Saussy has called the "workshop of equivalences": Do you have in your language a word for what we call . . . ?[30]

According to Tomio Tezuka, whose meeting with Heidegger in March 1954 provided the basis for the "Dialogue," Heidegger took much liberty with the contents of their conversation and made the Japanese term *Koto ba* sound much more in tune with his own philosophy.[31] But Heidegger is not solely to blame, and he has actually already sensed the pitfall in what is supposed to be a cross-cultural dialogue: "I now see still more clearly the danger that the language of our dialogue might constantly destroy the possibility of saying that of which we are speaking" (15). Heidegger suggests that German, the language used in their dialogue, has "obscured and shunted" the Japanese thinking "into a realm that is inappropriate to it" (14). Speaking the same language in such a dialogue runs the risk of totalization. Aggravating the danger is the fact that the Japanese interlocutor was already a student and an admirer of Heidegger's philosophy, a native informant who has already learned the tool of trade from the anthropologist and will thus provide "contaminated" data.

Despite the caveat against these perils, Heidegger's conclusion, ventriloquized through the voice of his interlocutor, is stunning: "As far as I am able to follow what you are saying, I sense a deeply concealed kinship with our thinking, precisely because your path of thinking and its language are so wholly other" (40–41). As Nancy and Levinas have suggested, Heidegger's obsession with Being as such has limited his contribution to the ethics of othering. Especially for Levinas, Heidegger's ontology is a philosophy of power and injustice because it "does not call into question the same" but instead "subordinates the relationship to the Other to the relation with Being in general," thus leading "inevitably to another power, to imperialist domination, to tyranny" (46–47). Just as Heidegger's conclusion demonstrates, the other is totalized into the kinship because it is reduced to the other of the same.

Studying the various forms of transpacific imaginations, I am interested in exploring a cross-cultural terrain where knowledge is replaced by "acknowledge," cognition by recognition. As a Chinese comparatist who now works mostly in English, I have been trying to figure out, not the Chinese equivalence to what may loosely be called the Western line of thinking about othering, but how to make sense of it in Chinese terms. Translation, as Saussy puts it, should not be seen "as a matter of finding equivalences between vocabularies but as one of making the meanings of one speech community mean something to another speech community"[32]—that's why the Heideggerian model of cross-cultural dialogue seems to have started on the wrong foot: He was looking for equivalences.

What Chinese terms may best translate Levinas's proposition for a face-to-face relationship, and what may make the best Chinese sense of Nancy's "disturbance of violent relatedness"? 認 (ren) is a Chinese word meaning "recognize, acknowledge, or establish (a relationship)." Etymologically, the word is made up of 言 (word) and 忍 (tolerate), literally meaning "to tolerate words (of the other)." The word has a ubiquitous presence in modern Chinese: it is part of 認識 (recognize), 認知 (epistemology), 承認 (acknowledge), 認親 (establish a relationship), and so on. 忍, the radical on the right, meaning "to tolerate, endure," is also equivalent to 能, meaning "ability." To summarize the implications of 認 in light of my explorations of transpacific interactions in this book: Just like Levinas's proposition that we listen to the Other's words rather than (dis)figure them, the meaning of 認 dictates that our ability to tolerate or endure the other's words should not precede our pretension to know the other. Before thematizing the meanings of the other, which to Levinas would amount to the violence of appropriation, we need to 認, or acknowledge the other.

Such seemingly nice matchmaking, however, carries risks on two levels. First, it may conflate ideas from different cultural traditions by ignoring factors that would have actually made them incompatible to each other. Levinas's ethics, for instance, is steeped in Judaic religiosity. Even though his profound critique of Christian figural reading of the Bible would have worked well with my own attempt to unpack the U.S. typological conceptions of the destiny of the Pacific—a running theme in my book—I hesitate to draw upon Levinas without qualification because what he means by "the other" may very well be quite other to me as an atheistic Chinese.

Second, whatever differences and similarities we may find in the process of matchmaking, we have to bear in mind that they emerge, as Saussy once reminded us, from our own comparative project; they should not be regarded as the "results of knowledge."[33] The meaning of 認 sounds Levinasian partly because I propose that one way in which we may live with our differences and similarities—across the Pacific or elsewhere—is to face language as ethical responsibility and possibility. An imperfect translation nonetheless generates meanings/functions for all the pieces that would make up a game—not just any game, but one of life and death, of literature and history, that has played out across the Pacific in the past centuries.

"What, sir," Mencius was once asked, "is your excellence?" And the Confucian sage answered: "我知言" (I understand language). It is certainly a long way to go from Confucian ethics and Chinese hermeneutics to the Western line of thinking about the other. But by putting them together, just like my assembling the diverse transpacific discourses in this book, I attempt to create a genealogy of counterpoetics that runs counter to self-centered, monological, and appropriative modes of literary representation and historical thinking. "When man truly approaches the Other," Levinas says, "he is uprooted from history" (52). Uprooting is significant and necessary because, as Edouard Glissant puts it, "The root is monolingual . . . Relation, by contrast, is spoken multilingually."[34]

On April 1, 2001, while doing reconnaissance in the South China Sea, a U.S. Navy spy plane collided with a Chinese military aircraft. The Chinese plane disappeared and its pilot was supposedly dead. The U.S. plane was also damaged and had to perform an emergency landing in China without authorization. The U.S. crew was detained by the Chinese, triggering a diplomatic crisis. What eventually resolved the issue was an intentional mistranslation, a purposeful realignment of the equivalence of words in English and Chinese as they are used in diplomatic exchanges. In his half-hearted letter of apology to the Chinese government, the U.S. ambassador Joseph W. Prueher states, "Please convey to the Chinese people and to the family of pilot Wang Wei that we are very sorry for their loss . . . We are very sorry the entering of China's airspace and the landing did not have verbal clearance."[35] When reported in Chinese media, however, the English phrase "very sorry," which sounds almost too simple or casual for an event of such magnitude, was translated into Chinese as 深表歉意 (shen biao qian yi). Meaning literally "expressing the deepest regret," the Chinese phrase carries a weight of formality that goes way beyond the English colloquial term. It was this Chinese phrase that was published in bold as headlines in Chinese media, and it effectively quieted the raging anti-U.S. sentiments. The crew was released and the spy plane returned. Despite the perennial U.S. complaint against China's pegging of its currency to the dollar, this is one pegged, uneven linguistic trade that the United States is more than happy to allow: "very sorry" for 深表歉意.

知言: understanding, not language, but languages.

Notes

Introduction

1. Charles Olson, *Call Me Ishmael* (1947; reprint, with a new afterword by Merton M. Sealts, Jr., Baltimore: Johns Hopkins University Press, 1997), 113–119.
2. F. O. Matthiessen, *American Renaissance: Art and Expression in the Age of Emerson and Whitman* (New York: Oxford University Press, 1941); Lawrance Thompson, *Melville's Quarrel with God* (Princeton, NJ: Princeton University Press, 1952); Charles Feidelson, Jr., *Symbolism and American Literature* (Chicago: University of Chicago Press, 1953); James L. Guetti, *The Limits of Metaphor: A Study of Melville, Conrad, and Faulkner* (Ithaca, NY: Cornell University Press, 1967); T. Walker Herbert, Jr., *Moby-Dick and Calvinism: A World Dismantled* (New Brunswick, NJ: Rutgers University Press, 1977); and Bainard Cowan, *Exiled Waters: Moby-Dick and the Crisis of Allegory* (Baton Rouge: Louisiana State University Press, 1982).
3. Olson, *Call Me Ishmael*; Stephen H. Sumida, *And the View from the Shore: Literary Traditions of Hawaii* (Seattle: University of Washington Press, 1991); William Spanos, *The Errant Art of Moby-Dick: The Canon, the Cold War, and the Struggle for American Studies* (Durham, NC: Duke University Press, 1995); John Carlos Rowe, *Literary Culture and U.S. Imperialism: From the Revolution to World War II* (New York: Oxford University Press, 2000); Amy Kaplan, *The Anarchy of Empire in the Making of U.S. Culture* (Cambridge, MA: Harvard University Press, 2002); David Palumbo-Liu, *Asian/American: Historical Crossings of a Racial Frontier* (Stanford, CA: Stanford University Press, 1999); and Rob Wilson, *Reimagining the American Pacific: From South Pacific to Bamboo Ridge and Beyond* (Durham, NC: Duke University Press, 2000).

4. Herman Melville, *Billy Budd and Other Stories,* introduction by Frederick Busch (New York: Penguin, 1986), 324; and Thomas Campbell, *The Poetical Works of Thomas Campbell,* ed. Rev. W. Alfred Hill (London: George Bell and Sons, 1891), 69.

5. Melville, *Billy Budd,* 323–324. Subsequent page references cited parenthetically in text.

6. Robert Borofsky, Introduction, in Robert Borofsky, ed., *Remembrance of Pacific Pasts: An Invitation to Remake History* (Honolulu: University of Hawaii Press, 2000), 4.

7. Claude Lévi-Strauss, *The Savage Mind* (London: Weidenfeld and Nicolson, 1966), 259–260.

8. Louis Althusser and Etienne Balibar, *Reading Capital,* trans. Ben Brewster (London: New Left Books, 1970), 99–100.

9. Henri Lefebvre, *The Production of Space,* trans. Donald Nicholson-Smith (Cambridge: Blackwell, 1991), 48. Subsequent page references cited parenthetically in text.

10. Lydia H. Liu, *The Clash of Empires: The Invention of China in Modern World Making* (Cambridge, MA: Harvard University Press, 2004), 2. Samuel P. Huntington, *The Clash of Civilizations and the Remaking of World Order* (New York: Simon and Schuster, 1996).

11. One of the most convincing readings in this regard has been done by Philip Fisher, *Still the New World: American Literature in a Culture of Creative Destruction* (Cambridge, MA: Harvard University Press, 1999). See also Michael T. Gilmore, *American Romanticism and the Marketplace* (Chicago: University of Chicago Press, 1985); and Rob Wilson, *American Sublime: The Genealogy of a Poetic Genre* (Madison: University of Wisconsin Press, 1991).

12. Samuel Taylor Coleridge, *Biographia Literaria; or, Biographical Sketches of My Literary Life and Opinions,* ed. George Watson (New York: Everyman's Library, 1956), 167.

13. Ralph Waldo Emerson, "Nature," in *Essays and Lectures* (New York: The Library of America, 1983), 10.

14. Emerson, "Self-Reliance," in *Essays and Lectures,* 271.

15. Wilson, *Reimagining the American Pacific,* 35.

16. James Clifford, "Valuing the Pacific—An Interview with James Clifford," in Borofsky, *Remembrance of Pacific Pasts,* 94.

17. Wilson, *Reimagining the American Pacific,* 34.

18. Arjun Appadurai, *Modernity at Large: Cultural Dimensions of Globalization* (Minneapolis: University of Minnesota Press, 1996), 4.

Part One: History

1. Sumida, *And the View from the Shore.*
2. Wilson, *Reimagining the American Pacific,* 103.
3. Arif Dirlik, "The Asia-Pacific Idea: Reality and Representation in the Invention of a Regional Structure," *Journal of World History* 3.1 (1992): 56.
4. Lefebvre, *The Production of Space.* See my introduction for a discussion of Lefebvre's concept of spatial production in relation to transpacific geopolitics.
5. Gilles Deleuze and Claire Parnet, *Dialogues,* trans. Hugh Tomlinson and Barbara Habberjam (New York: Columbia University Press, 1987), 9–10.
6. Ibid., 57.

1. Mark Twain

1. Mark Twain, *Letters from Hawaii,* ed. A. Grove Day (Honolulu: University of Hawaii Press, 1975), 271. Subsequent page references cited parenthetically in text.
2. Walter Francis Frear, *Mark Twain and Hawaii* (Chicago: Lakeside Press, 1947), 23.
3. The controversy finds best expression in the famous debate between Marshall Sahlins and Gananath Obeyesekere. See Marshall Sahlins, *Islands of History* (Chicago: University of Chicago Press, 1985) and *How "Natives" Think: About Captain Cook, for Example* (Chicago: University of Chicago Press, 1995); and Gananath Obeyesekere, *The Apotheosis of Captain Cook: European Mythmaking in the Pacific* (Princeton, NJ: Princeton University Press, 1992). The problem with such a debate, however, is that it leaves out the Pacific native perspectives. As Vilsoni Hereniko puts it, "Both Sahlins and Obeyesekere say their ultimate desire is that native voices be heard, but how can we hear those voices when they are screaming at each other so loudly?" (Vilsoni Hereniko, "Indigenous Knowledge and Academic Imperialism," in Borofsky, *Remembrance of Pacific Pasts,* 87).
4. Amy Kaplan, *The Anarchy of Empire in the Making of U.S. Culture* (Cambridge, MA: Harvard University Press, 2002), 69.
5. Mark Twain, *Following the Equator: A Journey around the World,* vol. 1 (1897; reprint, New York: Ecco Press, 1992), 30.
6. Twain, *Letters from Hawaii,* 111.
7. Kaplan, *Anarchy of Empire,* 87.
8. Nicholas Thomas, *Entangled Objects: Exchange, Material Culture, and Colonialism in the Pacific* (Cambridge, MA: Harvard University Press, 1991), 7–34.
9. Lefebvre, *The Production of Space,* 48. Sigmund Freud, *Civilization and Its Discontents,* in *The Freud Reader,* ed. Peter Gay (New York: W. W. Norton

and Company, 1989), 723. For a good discussion of "oceanic feeling" in the Pacific context, see Christopher Connery, "The Oceanic Feeling and the Regional Imaginary," in *Global/Local: Cultural Production and the Transnational Imaginary,* ed. Rob Wilson and Wimal Dissanayake (Durham, NC: Duke University Press, 1996), 284–311.

10. Lefebvre, *The Production of Space,* 308, 370.
11. Sumida, *And the View from the Shore,* 38–56.
12. Twain, *Letters from Hawaii,* 12.
13. I. C. Campbell, *A History of the Pacific Islands* (Berkeley: University of California Press, 1989), 151–152.
14. Twain, *Following the Equator,* 24–26.

2. Henry Adams

1. Henry Adams, *The Education of Henry Adams,* ed. Jean Gooder (New York: Penguin, 1995; hereafter cited as *EHA*).
2. Henry Adams, *The Letters of Henry Adams,* ed. J. C. Levenson et al. (Cambridge, MA: Harvard University Press, 1982), vol. III, 282 (hereafter cited as *Letters*).
3. Rowe, *Literary Culture and U.S. Imperialism,* 165–193. For Rowe's earlier work on Adams, see John Carlos Rowe, *Henry Adams and Henry James: The Emergence of a Modern Consciousness* (Ithaca, NY: Cornell University Press, 1976).
4. Palumbo-Liu, *Asian/American,* 31, 2.
5. Richard Drinnon, *Facing West: The Metaphysics of Indian-Hating and Empire-Building* (Minneapolis: University of Minnesota Press, 1980), 243–254.
6. Henry James, "The Beast in the Jungle," in *The Beast in the Jungle and Other Stories* (New York: Dover Publications, 1993), 66–67.
7. Henry James, *The Notebooks of Henry James,* ed. F. O. Matthiessen and Kenneth B. Murdock (Chicago: University of Chicago Press, 1981), 310–311.
8. In her introduction to the Penguin Classics edition of Adams's *Education,* the editor Jean Gooder also compares Adams to the male protagonist in the "Beast": "[Adams] was like Henry James's character, John Marcher, waiting in dread the spring of the 'beast' in his jungle, only to learn that he has misunderstood and lost the moment" (Jean Gooder, "Introduction," *EHA,* xxii).
9. T. J. Jackson Lears, *No Place of Grace: Antimodernism and the Transformation of American Culture, 1880–1920* (Chicago: University of Chicago Press, 1994), xi.
10. Percival Lowell, *The Soul of the Far East* (Boston: Houghton Mifflin, 1888), 1. For a detailed discussion of Lowell's ethnography of Japan, see my *Transpacific Displacement: Ethnography, Translation, and Intertextual Travel*

in *Twentieth-Century American Literature* (Berkeley: University of California Press, 2002), 26–32.

11. For a good summary of the development of the concept of childhood in the West, see Colin Heywood, *A History of Childhood: Children and Childhood in the West from Medieval to Modern Times* (Cambridge: Polity, 2001).

12. Rowe, *Henry Adams and Henry James,* 129; Joseph Riddel, "Reading America/American Readers," *Modern Language Notes* 99 (September 1984): 921–922; and Gregory Jay, *America the Scrivener: Deconstruction and the Subject of Literary History* (Ithaca, NY: Cornell University Press, 1990), 205.

13. Howard Horwitz, "*The Education* and the Salvation of History," in *New Essays on* The Education of Henry Adams, ed. John Carlos Rowe (Cambridge: Cambridge University Press, 1996), 143.

14. Ibid., 145.

15. R. P. Blackmur, *Henry Adams,* ed. and intro. Veronica A. Makowsky (New York: Da Capo Press, 1984), 248.

16. Sean Desmond Healy, *Boredom, Self, and Culture* (London: Associated University Press, 1984), 16.

17. Patricia Meyer Spacks, *Boredom: The Literary History of a State of Mind* (Chicago: University of Chicago Press, 1995), ix–x. Subsequent page references cited parenthetically in text.

18. Martha Banta, "Being a 'Begonia' in a Man's World," in Rowe, *New Essays on* The Education of Henry Adams, 53.

19. For a thoughtful discussion of modern secularized travel, see Johannes Fabian, *Time and the Other: How Anthropology Makes Its Object* (New York: Columbia University Press, 1983).

20. Elizabeth S. Goldstein, *Experience without Qualities: Boredom and Modernity* (Stanford, CA: Stanford University Press, 2005), 1.

21. Nicholas Thomas, *Entangled Objects: Exchange, Material Culture and Colonialism in the Pacific* (Cambridge, MA: Harvard University Press, 1991), 7–34.

22. Vanessa Smith, *Literary Culture and the Pacific: Nineteenth-Century Textual Encounters* (Cambridge: Cambridge University Press, 1998), 27–46.

23. Henry Adams, *Tahiti: Memoirs of Arii Taimai E Marama of Eimeo, Teriirere of Tooarai, Terrinui of Tahiti, Tauraatua I Amo* and *Memoirs of Marau Taaroa, Last Queen of Tahiti,* ed. and intro. Robert E. Spiller (1893 and 1901; reprint, New York: Scholars' Facsimiles and Reprints, 1947).

24. Bruce Mannheim and Dennis Tedlock, eds., *The Dialogic Emergence of Culture* (Urbana: University of Illinois Press, 1995), 1.

25. Smith, *Literary Culture and the Pacific,* 29, 31.

26. Jonathan Lamb, Vanessa Smith, and Nicholas Thomas, eds., *Exploration and Exchange: A South Seas Anthology, 1680–1900* (Chicago: University of Chicago Press, 2000), 318.

27. Daniel L. Manheim, "The Voice of Arii Taimai: Henry Adams and the Challenge of Empire." *Biography* 22.2 (Spring 1999): 222–223.
28. Banta, "Being a 'Begonia' in a Man's World," 55. See also Ernest Samuels, *Henry Adams* (Cambridge, MA: Harvard University Press, 1989), 199.
29. Walter J. Ong, *Orality and Literacy: The Technologizing of the Word* (New York: Routledge, 1982), 10.
30. Robert Louis Stevenson, *Collected Poems,* ed. Janet Adam Smith, 2nd ed. (New York: Viking Press, 1971), 181–209.
31. Bradford A. Booth and Ernest Mehew, eds., *The Letters of Robert Louis Stevenson,* vol. 7, September 1890–December 1892 (New Haven, CT: Yale University Press, 1995), 187.
32. Barry Menikoff, *Robert Louis Stevenson and* The Beach of Falesa (Stanford, CA: Stanford University Press, 1984), 72.
33. In his letter about *The Beach of Falesa,* Stevenson writes, "It is the first realistic South Seas Story; I mean with real South Sea Character and details of life; everybody else who has tried, that I have seen, got carried away by the romance and ended in a kind of sugar candy sham epic, and the whole effect was lost . . . Now I have got the smell and look of the thing a good deal. You will know more about the South Seas after you have read my little tale, than if you have read a library . . . everything, the life, the place, the dialects— trader's talk, which is a strange conglomerate of literary expressions and English and American slang, and Beach de Mar, or native English—the very trades and hopes and fears of the characters, are all novel and may be found unwelcome to that great, hulking, bullering whale, the public" (quoted in Menikoff, *Robert Louis Stevenson,* 12).
34. Robert Louis Stevenson, *A Footnote to History: Eight Years of Trouble in Samoa* (first published in 1892; Honolulu: University of Hawaii Press, 1996).
35. Quoted in Smith, *Literary Culture and the Pacific,* 213.
36. Smith, *Literary Culture and the Pacific,* 212.
37. Anthony Grafton, *The Footnote: A Curious History* (Cambridge, MA: Harvard University Press, 1997), back cover.
38. Smith, *Literary Culture and the Pacific,* 212.
39. Stevenson, *A Footnote to History,* xvii.
40. Quoted in Smith, *Literary Culture and the Pacific,* 193; my emphases.

3. Liang Qichao

1. Liang Qichao, "A Song of the Twentieth-Century Pacific," in *Xinmin congbao* (New citizen journal) 1 (1902): 109; unless otherwise stated, all translations from Liang's writings in Chinese are mine. If any indication of the historical significance of the poem to Liang's new geopolitical imagination,

he published it in the inaugural issue of the journal, which he founded and edited with the stated objectives of educating the people and promoting new cultural values.

2. Benjamin A. Elman, *From Philosophy to Philology: Intellectual and Social Aspects of Change in Late Imperial China* (Cambridge, MA: Harvard University Press, 1984), 6.

3. Joseph R. Levenson, "The Genesis of *Confucian China and Its Modern Fate*," in *The Historian's Workshop: Original Essays by Sixteen Historians,* ed. L. P. Curtis, Jr. (New York: Alfred A. Knopf, 1970), 288.

4. Liang Qichao, *Hanman lu* (Travels to Hawaii), in *Qingyi bao* (Pure discussion news) 35 (1900): Reprinted, 2276.

5. Leo Ou-fan Lee, *Shanghai Modern: The Flowering of a New Urban Culture in China, 1930–1945* (Cambridge, MA: Harvard University Press, 1999), 45.

6. Liang, *Hanman lu,* 2277–2279.

7. Liang Qichao, *Xin shixue* (New historiography), originally published in 1902; reprinted in *Liang Qichao shixue lunzhu sizhong* (Changsha, China: Yuelu shushe, 1998), 248–252. See also Xiaobing Tang, *Global Space and the Nationalist Discourse of Modernity: The Historical Thinking of Liang Qichao* (Stanford, CA: Stanford University Press, 1996), 64–65.

8. Tang, *Global Space,* 27–28.

9. Walter Benjamin, *The Origin of German Tragic Drama,* trans. John Osborne (New York: Verso, 1998), 177.

10. Ibid., 179.

11. Liang, "A Song of the Twentieth-Century Pacific," 110–111.

12. Liang Qichao, *Xindalu youji* (Notes from a journey to the new continent) (Originally published in 1904; reprinted, Changsha, China: Hunan renmin chubanshe, 1981), 10–13. The English original is from *California Addresses of President Roosevelt* (San Francisco: California Promotion Committee, 1903), 95–97.

13. Bruce Cumings, "Rimspeak; or, The Discourse of the 'Pacific Rim,'" in Arif Dirlik, ed., *What Is in a Rim? Critical Perspectives on the Pacific Region Idea* (Lanham, MD: Rowan & Littlefield, 1998), 54, 59.

14. Liang, *Xindalu youji,* 14–15. The English translation, with modification, is from Leo Ou-fan Lee and David Arkush, trans. and eds., *Land without Ghosts: Chinese Impressions of America from the Mid-Nineteenth Century to the Present* (Berkeley and Los Angeles: University of California Press, 1989), 89.

15. Jianhua Chen, "Chinese 'Revolution' in the Syntax of World Revolution," in *Tokens of Translation: The Problem of Translation in Global Circulations,* ed. Lydia H. Liu (Durham, NC: Duke University Press, 1999), 366–370. See also Prasenjit Duara, *Rescuing History from the Nation: Questioning Narratives of Modern China* (Chicago: University of Chicago Press, 1995), 126.

16. Liang, *Hanman lu,* 2280–2283. Translation is from Chen, "Chinese 'Revolution,'" 366; italics mine.

17. Liang, *Hanman lu,* 2281. Translation is from J. D. Schmidt, *Within the Human Realm: The Poetry of Huang Zunxian, 1848–1905* (Cambridge: Cambridge University Press, 1994), 58.

18. Liang also proposed a "prose revolution," as he recorded in his transpacific journal: "Tokutomi is one of the three chief newspaper editors in Japan. His literary style is as sharp as it is powerful, uniting European thought with Japanese prose writings in a perfect style. He has really created a new prose genre. I admire him very much. If China should have a prose revolution, it must start at this level" (*Hanman lu,* 2349; translation is from Chen, "Chinese 'Revolution,'" 367). But his overall idea for prose revolution is quite sketchy and not as significant as his for poetic and historiographical revolutions.

19. Liang, *Xin shixue,* 244, 246–247. Translation is from Tang, *Global Space,* 63–64.

20. Liang, *Hanman lu,* 2479.

21. Liang Qichao, "Yanjiu wenhuashide jige zhongyao wenti" (Important issues in the study of cultural history; 1922); reprinted, Xia Xiaohong, ed., *Liang Qichao wenxuan* (Selected works of Liang Qichao; Beijing: Zhongguo guangbo dianshi chubanshe, 1992), Vol. 1, 553.

22. Lefebvre, *The Production of Space,* 373, 397.

23. Bruce Cumings, *Parallax Visions: Making Sense of American–East Asian Relations at the End of the Century* (Durham, NC: Duke University Press, 1999), 1.

24. Lefebvre, *Production of Space,* 397.

Part Two: Literature

1. Herman Melville, *Moby-Dick; or, The Whale,* ed. Harrison Hayford, Hershel Parker, and G. Thomas Tanselle, Northwestern-Newberry Edition (Evanston, IL: Northwestern University Press and the Newberry Library, 1988), 482 (hereafter cited as *MD*).

2. For a reading of Melville's geopolitics as demonstrated in Ishmael's cartography, see Russell Reising and Peter J. Kvidera, "Fast Fish and Raw Fish: *Moby-Dick,* Japan, and Melville's Thematics of Geography," *New England Quarterly* 70.2 (1997): 285–305.

3. For examples of canonical symbolist readings of *Moby-Dick,* see Matthiessen, *American Renaissance*; Thompson, *Melville's Quarrel with God*; Feidelson, *Symbolism and American Literature*; Guetti, *The Limits of Metaphor*; Herbert, *Moby-Dick and Calvinism: A World Dismantled*; Cowan, *Exiled Waters.*

4. Sumida, *And the View from the Shore*; Spanos, *The Errant Art of* Moby-Dick; Rowe, *Literary Culture and U.S. Imperialism*; Wilson, *Reimagining the American Pacific*.

4. Collecting in the Pacific

1. Arrell Morgan Gibson, *Yankee in Paradise: The Pacific Basin Frontier,* completed with the assistance of John S. Whitehead (Albuquerque: University of New Mexico Press, 1993), 172–173, 97–101.
2. Olson, *Call Me Ishmael,* 23.
3. Ibid., 18.
4. Ibid., 24.
5. Gilmore, *American Romanticism and the Marketplace,* 118; Paul Royster, "Melville's Economy of Language," in *Ideology and Classic American Literature,* ed. Sacvan Bercovitch and Myra Jehlen (Cambridge: Cambridge University Press, 1986), 313; and Wai-chee Dimock, *Empire for Liberty: Melville and the Poetics of Individualism* (Princeton, NJ: Princeton University Press, 1989), 3–41. See also Rowe, *Literary Culture and U.S. Imperialism,* 77–96; and Wilson, *Reimagining the American Pacific,* 81–83.
6. Karl Marx, *Pre-Capitalist Economic Formations,* trans. Jack Cohen (New York: International Publishers, 1965), 67–120.
7. Karl Marx, *Capital: A Critique of Political Economy,* trans. Samuel Moore and Edward Aveling (New York: The Modern Library, 1965), 784–787.
8. Jean Baudrillard, *The Mirror of Production,* trans. Mark Poster (St. Louis, MO: Telos Press, 1975), 86–87. See also Michel Foucault, *The Order of Things: An Archaeology of the Human Sciences* (New York: Vintage Books, 1973), 221–226.
9. I am quoting from Michael Steinberg, "The Collector as Allegorist: Goods, Gods, and Objects of History," in Michael Steinbury, ed., *Walter Benjamin and the Demand of History* (Ithaca, NY: Cornell University Press, 1996), 114. Steinberg's version reads a bit more clearly than what is in the complete translation by Howard Eiland and Kevin McLaughlin of Walter Benjamin, *The Arcades Project,* trans. Howard Eiland and Kevin McLaughlin (Cambridge, MA: Harvard University Press, 1999), 204–205.
10. Jean Baudrillard, *The System of Objects,* trans. James Benedict (London: Verso, 1996), 95.
11. Walter Benjamin, "Unpacking My Library: A Talk about Collecting," in *Selected Writings,* vol. 2, trans. Rodney Livingston et al., ed. Michael W. Jennings, Howard Eiland, and Gary Smith (Cambridge, MA: Harvard University Press, 1999), 488; italics mine.

12. Herman Melville, "A Thought on Book-Binding," in *The Piazza Tales and Other Prose Pieces, 1839–1860,* ed. Harrison Hayford, Alma A. MacDougall, G. Thomas Tanselle, and others, Northwestern-Newberry Edition (Evanston, IL: Northwestern University Press and the Newberry Library, 1987), 237–238.
13. Marx, *Capital,* 618–620.
14. Georges Bataille, *Visions of Excess: Selected Writings, 1927–1939,* ed. and trans. Allan Stoekl (Minneapolis: University of Minnesota Press, 1985), 118.
15. Howard Eiland and Kevin McLaughlin, Translators' Foreword to Walter Besnjamin, *Arcades Project,* xii.

5. Ahab's Collectibles

1. Michael Paul Rogin, *Subversive Genealogy: The Politics and Art of Herman Melville* (Berkeley: University of California Press, 1979), 118. See also Paul McCarthy, *"The Twisted Mind": Madness in Herman Melville's Fiction* (Iowa City: University of Iowa Press, 1990), 52–53.
2. Herman Melville, *Correspondence,* ed. Lynn Horth, Northwestern-Newberry Edition (Evanston, IL: Northwestern University Press and the Newberry Library, 1991), 192.
3. Herman Melville, *Redburn* (New York: Penguin Books, 1976), 143.
4. In Balzac's novel *Cousin Pons,* the protagonist Sylvain Pons is an eccentric antiquarian collector (in whom we see, partly by the phonetic proximity of names, the shadow of another antiquarian collector, Mrs. Gereth in Henry James's *The Spoils of Poynton*). Melville owned a copy of the English translation (by Katherine Prescott Wormeley) of Balzac's novel, in which he marked a number of pages, including this sentence spoken by Pons: "they were the flower of my collection." See Walker Cowan, *Melville's Marginalia,* ed. Stephen Orgel (New York: Garland, 1987), 1:124.
5. For studies that compare Ahab and Kurtz, see Guetti, *Limits of Metaphor;* and David Simpson, *Fetishism and Imagination: Dickens, Melville, Conrad* (Baltimore: Johns Hopkins University Press, 1982).
6. Joseph Conrad, *Heart of Darkness* (1899; reprint, ed. Robert Kimbrough, Norton Critical Edition, 3rd ed., New York: W. W. Norton, 1988), 57.
7. Feidelson, *Symbolism and American Literature,* 32–34; Gilmore, *American Romanticism and the Marketplace,* 127–128; and Royster, "Melville's Economy of Language," 316–319. These scholars have inherited, perhaps justifiably so, mid-nineteenth-century America's fascination with the nature of the symbol (Hawthorne, Poe, and Melville).
8. Svetlana Boym, *The Future of Nostalgia* (New York: Basic Books, 2001), 10.

9. Susan Stewart, *On Longing: Narratives of the Miniature, the Gigantic, the Souvenir, the Collection* (Durham, NC: Duke University Press, 1993), 133.

10. Melville, *Correspondence*, 191.

11. Herman Melville, *Typee: A Peep at Polynesian Life* (1846; reprint, New York: Penguin Books, 1996), 126.

12. In the *Oxford English Dictionary*, the first recorded use of *blackbirding* is from 1873, but the practice had existed long before that. See Gibson, *Yankee in Paradise*, 167–169.

13. I. C. Campbell, *A History of the Pacific Islands*, 111.

14. Marx, *Capital*, 185–196.

15. Baudrillard, *Mirror of Production*, 95; italics original.

16. Karl Marx and Frederick Engels, *The Communist Manifesto* (New York: Pathfinder, 1970), 19.

17. Herman Melville, "Bartleby, the Scrivener: A Story of Wall-Street," in *Piazza Tales and Other Prose Pieces*, 33.

18. Baudrillard, *Mirror of Production*, 44.

6. Ishmael, a Pacific Historian

1. For the former, narratology-centered reading, see Spanos, *Errant Art*; and for the latter, personality-based reading, see Mathiessen, *American Renaissance*.

2. B. Cowan, *Exiled Waters*, 63.

3. Melville, *Redburn*, 178.

4. Oscar Handlin, *Truth in History* (Cambridge, MA: Harvard University Press, 1979), 53–56.

5. For an overview of the paradigmatic shift in historiography, see Arnaldo Momigliano, *The Classical Foundations of Modern Historiography* (Berkeley: University of California Press, 1990), 54–79; and Arnaldo Momigliano, *Studies in Historiography* (New York: Harper and Row, 1966), 1–39. See also Foucault, *Order of Things*.

6. Momigliano, *Studies in Historiography*, 3.

7. Momigliano, *Classical Foundations*, 54.

8. Ernest Breisach, *Historiography: Ancient, Medieval, and Modern*, 2nd ed. (Chicago: University of Chicago Press, 1994); Herbert Butterfield, *The Whig Interpretation of History* (New York: W. W. Norton, 1965); and Trevor Colbourn, *The Lamp of Experience: Whig History and the Intellectual Origins of the American Revolution* (1965; reprint, Indianapolis: Liberty Fund, 1998). The striking lack of mention of antiquarianism in the works of canonical American historians like Perry Miller is a symptom of the successful replacement of antiquarian approaches to history by the nineteenth-century philosophical paradigm.

9. Butterfield, *Whig Interpretation*, v.
10. Alexis de Tocqueville, *Democracy in America*, trans. George Lawrence, ed. J. P. Mayer (New York: Perennial Classics, 2000), 493–496.
11. Melville, *Redburn*, 215.
12. The editors of the Northwestern-Newberry edition of *Moby-Dick* think that these two terms could be either "Traders' Pidgin" or "Melville's own invention" (*MD* 816).
13. Max Weber, *The Protestant Ethic and the Spirit of Capitalism*, trans. Talcott Parsons (London: George Allen & Unwin, 1930).
14. W. Cowan, *Melville's Marginalia*, 1:525.
15. Leo Bersani, *The Culture of Redemption* (Cambridge, MA: Harvard University Press, 1990), 136–154.
16. For a poststructuralist reading of Ishmael's cetology as writing, see Rodolphe Gasché, "The Scene of Writing: A Deferred Outset," *Glyph* 1 (1977): 150–171.
17. David Levin, *History as Romantic Art: Bancroft, Prescott, Motley, and Parkman* (Stanford, CA: Stanford University Press, 1959); and Handlin, *Truth in History*, 56–58.
18. Ralph Waldo Emerson, *Essays and Lectures* (New York: The Library of America, 1983), 240. Maybe I am catching the worst (but many will surely consider the best) moment in Emerson's thinking about history. Emerson seems in this instance carried away by his own rhetorical hyperbole, for he is actually not so uninterested in historical facts (see Eduardo Cadava, *Emerson and the Climate of History* [Stanford, CA: Stanford University Press, 1997]). Even so, there is little question that Emerson's thinking represents, and to a large extent shapes, a general trend in nineteenth-century philosophical historicism that disregards antiquarianism.
19. Melville, "Bartleby," 20. Subsequent page references cited parenthetically in text.

7. Queequeg, the Pacific Man

1. Elizabeth Renker, *Striking through the Mask: Herman Melville and the Scene of Writing* (Baltimore: Johns Hopkins University Press, 1996), xviii.
2. Patricia Cline Cohen, *A Calculating People: The Spread of Numeracy in Early America* (New York: Routledge, 1999), ix.
3. Quoted in ibid., 3.
4. Rogin, *Subversive Genealogy*, 19; and Samuel Otter, *Melville's Anatomy* (Berkeley: University of California Press, 2000).
5. Melville, *Correspondence*, 191.
6. Olson, *Call Me Ishmael*, 104.

7. Susan Howe, *The Birth-mark: Unsettling the Wilderness in American Literary History* (Hanover, NH: University Press of New England, 1993), 181.

8. Ibid.

9. Olson, *Call Me Ishmael,* 113–119.

10. For an interesting study of the historical (not merely symbolic) process in which indigenous Pacific Islanders have appropriated Euro-American cultures, see Thomas, *Entangled Objects,* 83–124.

8. Melville's Pacific Becoming

1. D. H. Lawrence, *Studies in Classic American Literature* (1922; reprint, New York: Doubleday, 1953), 146.

2. Melville, *Typee,* 2.

3. Elizabeth Grosz, ed., *Becomings: Explorations in Time, Memory, and Futures* (Ithaca, NY: Cornell University Press, 1999), 4.

4. Emerson, *Essays and Lectures,* 403–404. For a reading of Emerson's circle as a pronouncement of enterprise capitalism, see Fisher, *Still the New World.*

5. Hershel Parker, *Herman Melville: A Biography,* vol. 1 (Baltimore: Johns Hopkins University Press, 1996), 694.

6. Renker, *Striking through the Mask,* xvii.

7. Melville, *Correspondence,* 139.

8. The statements of Melville's account with Harper and Brothers show that between April 10, 1847, and November 16, 1848, Melville purchased three identical copies of the Harper 1846 or later edition of the Webster dictionary. By comparing the balance in Melville's account and the listed price for the dictionary in the Harper catalogue, Merton M. Sealts, Jr., has ruled out the 1847 Goodrich revision of Webster as Melville's purchase (Sealts, *Melville's Reading,* revised and enlarged edition [Columbia: University of South Carolina Press, 1988], 225). Hence, I choose to rely on the 1846 edition, which was published closest to the date of Melville's first purchase.

9. Melville, *Correspondence,* 114.

10. Renker, *Striking through the Mask,* 88.

11. James William Nechas, *Synonomy, Repetition, and Restatement in the Vocabulary of Herman Melville's Moby-Dick* (Norwood, PA: Norwood Editions, 1978), 22–23.

12. Herman Melville, *Pierre; or, The Ambiguities,* ed. Harrison Hayford, Hershel Parker, and G. Thomas Tanselle, Northwestern-Newberry Edition (Evanston, IL: Northwestern University Press and the Newberry Library, 1971), 244.

13. Ibid.

14. Lawrence Buell, "Melville the Poet," in *The Cambridge Companion to Herman Melville,* ed. Robert S. Levine (Cambridge: Cambridge University

Press, 1998), 135–136; Nina Baym, "Melville's Quarrel with Fiction," *PMLA* 94 (1979): 909–923.

15. Buell, "Melville the Poet," 135.
16. Just as philosophical historiography replaced antiquarianism in the nineteenth century, literary criticism since the Romantic movement has also preoccupied itself with disinterestedness and truth, denying its own inherent antiquarianism. Deprived of their pretense to truth-seeking, literary critics are quintessential antiquarians who collect and assemble textual fragments to create a self-serving system of meaning. This is a topic to be addressed elsewhere; but for insightful discussion of similar issues, see Jerome J. McGann, *The Romantic Ideology: A Critical Investigation* (Chicago: University Of Chicago Press, 1983); and Charles Bernstein, *My Way* (Chicago: University of Chicago Press, 1999), 36–51.
17. Herbert, *Moby-Dick and Calvinism*; Thompson, *Melville's Quarrel with God*; Michael J. Colacurcio, *Doctrine and Difference: Essays in the Literature of New England* (New York: Routledge, 1997), 237–241; and Howe, *Birth-mark*, 11–12.
18. W. Cowan, *Melville's Marginalia*, 1:526. Emerson himself also has a complicated relationship to antinomianism; see Perry Miller's seminal essay "From Edwards to Emerson," in *Errand into the Wilderness* (Cambridge, MA: Harvard University Press, 1956), 184–203; and Wesley T. Mott, "Emerson and Antinomianism: The Legacy of the Sermons," *American Literature* 50.3 (1978): 369–397.
19. Quoted in Howe, *Birth-mark*, 11.
20. Samuel Taylor Coleridge, *Biographia Literaria; or, Biographical Sketches of My Literary Life and Opinions*, ed. George Watson (New York: Everyman's Library, 1956), 167.
21. Ibid.
22. Ibid.
23. Melville, *Correspondence*, 162; italics mine.
24. Walter Benjamin, "Fate and Character," in *Selected Writings*, vol. 1, ed. Marcus Bullock and Michael W. Jennings (Cambridge, MA: Harvard University Press, 1996), 201–206.
25. For Melville's markings in his copies of Emerson's "Fate" and "Character," see W. Cowan, *Melville's Marginalia*, 1:518, 527–528.
26. Emerson, *Essays and Lectures*, 946, 495, 948.
27. Ibid., 958.

Part Three: Counterpoetics

1. Palumbo-Liu, *Asian/American*, 218.
2. Ibid., 239.

9. The Poetics of Error

1. Gayatri Chakravorty Spivak, "Can the Subaltern Speak?," in *Marxism and the Interpretation of Culture,* ed. Cary Nelson and Lawrence Grossberg (Urbana: University of Illinois Press, 1988), 271–313.

2. Him Mark Lai, Genny Lim, and Judy Yung, eds. and trans., *Island: Poetry and History of Chinese Immigrants on Angel Island, 1910–1940* (originally published in 1980; Seattle: University of Washington Press, 1991), 9–10 (hereafter cited as *Island*).

3. Te-hsing Shan, "Angel Island Poetry," in *Multilingual Anthology of American Literature,* ed. Werner Sollors and Marc Shell (New York: New York University Press, 2000), 577–581, 729–731. For a longer version of Shan's essay (in Chinese), see his " 'Yi wo ailun ru quanwo': Tianshidao beigede mingke yu zaixian" (" 'I am ashamed to be curled up like a worm on Island': Inscription and Representation in Angel Island Poetry"), in He Wenjing and Shan Te-hsing, ed., *Zaixian zhengzhi yu huayi meiguo wenxue* (The politics of representation and Chinese-American literature; Taipei, Taiwan: Zhongyang Yajiuyuan Omei Yanjiusuo, 1996), 1–56.

4. The English translation of this poem is taken from my own book, *Shi: A Radical Reading of Chinese Poetry* (New York: Roof Books, 1997), 37.

5. Richard E. Strassberg, *Inscribed Landscapes: Travel Writing from Imperial China* (Berkeley: University of California Press, 1994), 11.

6. Luo Zongtao, "Tangren tibishi chutan" (A preliminary study of tibishi of the Tang dynasty), *Zhonghua wenshi luncong* 47 (1991): 153–183. In English, Judith T. Zeitline's recent essay, "Disappearing Verses: Writing on Walls and Anxieties of Loss," contains wonderful case studies of tibishi (Judith T. Zeitline and Lydia H. Liu, eds., *Writing and Materiality in China: Essays in Honor of Patrick Hanan* [Cambridge, MA: Harvard University Press, 2003]), 73–132.

7. Sau-ling C. Wong, "The Politics and Poetics of Folksong Reading: Literary Portrayals of Life under Exclusion," in *Entry Denied: Exclusion and the Chinese Community in America, 1882–1943,* ed. Sucheng Chan (Philadelphia: Temple University Press, 1991), 253.

8. In my book *Transpacific Displacement* (2002), I study a similar case in which Chinese poetry is often treated thematically by the English translators who ignore the politics of the poetic form. See Chapter 6 of the book, 164–182.

9. Gilles Deleuze and Félix Guattari, *Kafka: Toward a Minor Literature,* trans. Dana Polan (Minneapolis: University of Minnesota Press, 1986), 23.

10. Masao Miyoshi, *Off Center: Power and Culture Relations between Japan and the United States* (Cambridge, MA: Harvard University Press, 1991), 28.

11. Ibid., 36.

12. Stephen Owen, *Readings in Chinese Literary Thought* (Cambridge, MA: Harvard University Press, 1992), 40.

13. Pauline Yu, *The Reading of Imagery in the Chinese Poetic Tradition* (Princeton, NJ: Princeton University Pres, 1987), 32.

14. There has been a very useful debate in Chinese studies over the exact nature of such comparisons. Scholars such as Stephen Owen, Pauline Yu, and François Jullien would take the alleged cultural differences as givens or results of knowledge, whereas Haun Saussy and Longxi Zhang have expressed skepticism over such contrasts. Saussy, for instance, argues that "if the Chinese thinkers are the antithesis (or the antidote) of the Greeks, it is we who make them so . . . The lack emerges from a comparative project" (*The Great Walls of Discourse and Other Adventures in Cultural China* [Cambridge, MA: Harvard University Press, 2001], 113). Saussy's earlier work, *The Problem of a Chinese Aesthetic* (Stanford, CA: Stanford University Press, 1993), is one of the best studies of the term *shi yan zhi*. I will address this issue of contrast in the conclusion of this book.

15. Owen, *Readings in Chinese Literary Thought*, 27.

16. Dick Hebdige, *Subculture: The Meaning of Style* (London: Routledge, 1979), 3.

17. Susan Stewart, *Crimes of Writing: Problems in the Containment of Representation* (New York: Oxford University Press, 1991), 212.

18. Madeline Yuan-yin Hsu, *Dreaming of Gold, Dreaming of Home: Transnationalism and Migration between the United States and China, 1882–1943* (Stanford, CA: Stanford University Press, 2000), 75.

19. Chinese Exclusion Case Files #21685/1–16. Quoted in Hsu, *Dreaming of Gold*, 70.

20. Aristotle, *Poetics*, trans. S. H. Butcher (New York: Hill and Wang, 1961), XXV.5.

21. Stewart, *Crimes of Writing*, 228.

22. "Carved on the Walls: Poetry by Early Chinese Immigrants," in Paul Lauter, general ed., *The Heath Anthology of American Literature*, 5th ed., Vol. D (Boston: Houghton Mifflin Company, 2006), 1873–1881. This section of the anthology is selected from *Island*, whose editors provided the headnotes for the anthology.

10. Legends from Camp

1. Lawson Fusao Inada, "Shrinking the Pacific," in "Asia/Pacific as a Space of Cultural Production," special issue of *boundary 2* 21.1 (1994): 57–58.

2. Wilson, *Reimagining the American Pacific*, 95.

3. Lawson Fusao Inada, *Legends from Camp* (Minneapolis: Coffee House Press, 1993), 3 (hereafter cited as *Legends*).

4. Michel de Certeau, *The Writing of History*, trans. Tom Conley (New York: Columbia University Press, 1988), 35.

5. On the copyright page of *Legends,* this photo is identified as "Camp photo c. 1944 by the author's uncle, Corporal Tom Saito, visiting on furlough."
6. D. W. Winnicott, *Playing and Reality* (London: Tavistock Publications, 1971), 1–25.
7. Friedrich Nietzsche, "On the Uses and Disadvantages of History for Life," in *Untimely Meditations,* ed. Daniel Breazeale, trans. R. J. Hollingdale (Cambridge: Cambridge University Press, 1997), 68–69.
8. Ibid., 73.
9. Ibid., 75.
10. Benjamin, *Origin of German Tragic Drama,* 178.
11. Ibid., 177–178.
12. Ibid., 179.
13. Michel Foucault, *Power/Knowledge: Selected Interviews and Other Writings, 1972–1977* (New York: Pantheon, 1980), 149.
14. Lefebvre, *The Production of Space,* 285.

11. Mapping Histories

1. Theresa Hak Kyung Cha, *Dictee* (Berkeley: University of California Press, 2001), frontispiece. Subsequent page references cited parenthetically in text.
2. Laura Hyun Yi Kang, "The 'Liberatory Voice' of Theresa Hak Kyung Cha's *Dictee,*" in *Writing Self, Writing Nation: A Collection of Essays on* Dictee *by Theresa Hak Kyung Cha,* ed. Laura Hyun Yi Kang et al. (Berkeley: Third Woman Press, 1994), 99.
3. Juliana Spahr, *Everybody's Autonomy: Connective Reading and Collective Identity* (Tuscaloosa: University of Alabama Press, 2001), 124.
4. Ibid.,122.
5. Mary Ann Caws, *The Art of Interference: Stressed Readings in Verbal and Visual Texts* (Princeton, NJ: Princeton University Press, 1989), 3.
6. Naoki Sakai, *Translation and Subjectivity: On "Japan" and Cultural Nationalism* (Minneapolis: University of Minnesota Press, 1997), 25.
7. Ki-baik Lee, *A New History of Korea,* trans. Edward W. Wagner and Edward J. Shultz (Cambridge, MA: Harvard University Press, 1984), 313.
8. Anne Anlin Cheng, *The Melancholy of Race: Psychoanalysis, Assimilation, and Hidden Grief* (New York: Oxford University Press, 2000), 143.
9. Susan Sontag, *On Photography* (New York: Dell, 1977), 57.
10. W. G. Sebald, *On the Natural History of Destruction,* trans. Anthea Bell (New York: Random House, 2003), 98.
11. Jacques Derrida, *Archive Fever: A Freudian Impression,* trans. Eric Prenowitz (Chicago: University of Chicago Press, 1996), 18.

12. Theresa Hak Kyung Cha, ed., *Apparatus, Cinematographic Apparatus: Selected Writings* (New York: Tanam Press, 1981), Preface (unpaginated).

13. I am indebted to Walter Lew for identifying the visual resemblance between the two images when he gave an unpublished paper at the Cross-Cultural Poetics Conference in Minneapolis in 1997. Lew's *Excerpts from, Dikte=dikte: For Dictee (1982)* (Seoul, Korea: Yeul Eum Publishing, 1992) is one of the best poetic and critical engagements with Cha's work.

14. J. Hillis Miller, *Topographies* (Stanford, CA: Stanford University Press, 1995), 5.

15. Today the naming of the sea and the territorial claim to the Dokto Islets still cause much tension between Japan and Korea.

16. The politics of naming on Cha's map may also be explored with respect to the name "Yellow Sea" (a Chinese name), which is also called "West Sea." But the relationship between China and Korea is quite different from the one between Japan and Korea.

17. Derrida, *Archive Fever,* 36.

Conclusion

1. T. S. Eliot, introduction to Ezra Pound, *Selected Poems* (London: Faber and Faber, 1928), xvi.

2. Georg Wilhelm Friedrich Hegel, *The Philosophy of History,* trans. J. Sibree (New York: Dover, 1956), 102–103.

3. For an excellent reading of Hegel and China, see the chapter entitled "Hegel's Chinese Imagination" in Saussy, *Problem of a Chinese Aesthetic,* 151–184.

4. The best example of postmodernist claims for the fictional or discursive nature of historical knowledge can be found in Hayden White, *Metahistory: The Historical Imagination in Nineteenth-Century Europe* (Baltimore: Johns Hopkins University Press, 1973).

5. Roger Chartier, *On the Edge of the Cliff: History, Language, and Practices,* trans. Lydia G. Cochrane (Baltimore: Johns Hopkins University Press, 1997), 20.

6. *Asashi Shimbun* (August 9, 1997) 1; my translation.

7. A partial list of such reviews, articles, and conference papers might include Emily Nussbaum, "Turning Japanese: The Hiroshima Poetry Hoax," *Lingua Franca* (November 1996): 82–84; Marjorie Perloff, "In Search of the Authentic Other: The Poetry of Araki Yasusada," *Boston Review* 22.2 (1997), www.bostonreview.net/BR22.2/BR22.2.html (accessed July 15, 2005); Eliot Weinberger, "On Yasusada: Can I Get a Witness?" *Jacket* 5 (October 1998), www.jacketmagazine.com/05/yasu-wein.html (accessed July 15, 2005); Ju-

liana Chang et al., "Displacements," *Boston Review* 22.3 (1997), www
.bostonreview.net/BR22.3/BR22.3.html (accessed July 15, 2005); Charles
Bernstein, "Fraud's Phantom: A Brief yet Unreliable Accounting of Fighting
Fraud with Fraud (No Pun on Freud Intended), with Special Reference to
White Male Rage," MLA presentation, December 29, 2000; and Eric Hayot,
"The Strange Case of Araki Yasusada: Author, Object," *PMLA* 120.1 (2005):
66–81. Most of the Internet discussions are archived at SUNY-Buffalo's Poetics Discussion List, www.listserv.acsu.buffalo.edu/archives/poetics.html
(accessed July 22, 2005).

8. See the front matter and back cover blurbs in Araki Yasusada, *Doubled Flowering: From the Notebooks of Araki Yasusada* (New York: Roof Books, 1997).

9. Akitoshi Nagahata, "Argument over a Fictitious Atomic Bomb Survivor
Poet," *Asashi Shimbun* (August 14, 1997): 7; my translation.

10. Perloff, "In Search of the Authentic Other," 157.

11. Gayatri Chakravorty Spivak, *Death of a Discipline* (New York: Columbia
University Press, 2003), 26. Subsequent page references cited parenthetically in text.

12. Mikhail Epstein, "Letter to Tosa Motokiyu," in Araki, *Doubled Flowering*,
135–136.

13. Bill Freind, "Hoaxes and Heteronymity: An Interview with Kent Johnson,"
Vert 5 (2002), www.litvert.com/KJ_Interview.html (accessed July 22, 2005).

14. K. K. Ruthven, *Faking Literature* (New York: Cambridge University Press,
2001), 25–27.

15. Quoted in Perloff, "In Search of the Authentic Other," 155.

16. Lisa Yoneyama, *Hiroshima Traces: Time, Space, and the Dialectics of Memory*
(Berkeley: University of California Press, 1999), 87–88.

17. Cathy Caruth, *Unclaimed Experience: Trauma, Narrative, and History* (Baltimore: Johns Hopkins University Press, 1996), 18.

18. Yoneyama, *Hiroshima Traces*, 15.

19. Araki, *Doubled Flowering*, 15.

20. Yoneyama, *Hiroshima Traces*, 3.

21. Bernstein, "Fraud's Phantom," 4, 10. To provide a longer quote from Bernstein's powerful critique: "The literary frauds of Sokol, MacAuley and
Stewart, and Johnson are not critiques of moral discourse, that is, attacks on
the social codes of honesty and integrity; on the contrary, these frauds were
used as a way of shoring up moral discourse against the perceived relativism
of contemporary culture. These authors embraced fraud not in a joyous or
comic dance with the improbabilities or insufficiencies of authenticity but
rather out of a sense of moral outrage—specifically of white male rage . . .
Doubled Flowering represents the apotheosis of the poetics of resentment in
the 1990s—resentment against the apparent new entitlements to those

often invisible or inaudible in previous representations of contemporary literature, resentment that is to feminism, gay rights, and multiculturalism as arbiters of literary taste" (4–10).

22. Ezra Pound, *Literary Essays of Ezra Pound,* ed. and intro. T. S. Eliot (London: Faber and Faber, 1954), 4; italics mine.

23. Emmanuel Levinas, *Totality and Infinity: An Essay on Exteriority,* trans. Alphonso Lingis (Pittsburgh, PA: Duquesne University Press, 1969), 197. Subsequent page references cited parenthetically in text.

24. Sam Knight, "An Anxious Morning on the Tube, Then a Man Shot Dead," *Times Online,* www.timesonline.co.uk/tol/news/uk/article546911.ece (accessed October 23, 2007).

25. Jean-Luc Nancy, *Being Singular Plural,* trans. Robert D. Richardson and Anne E. O'Byrne (Stanford, CA: Stanford University Press, 2000), 30, 7, 93.

26. Jill Robbins, *Altered Reading: Levinas and Literature* (Chicago: University of Chicago Press, 1999), 18.

27. Martin Heidegger, *Being and Time,* trans. John Macquarrie and Edward Robinson (New York: Harper, 1962), 161.

28. Martin Heidegger, "A Dialogue on Language: Between a Japanese and an Inquirer," in Martin Heidegger, *On the Way to Language,* trans. Peter D. Hertz (San Francisco: Harper and Row, 1971), 23. Subsequent page references cited parenthetically in text.

29. Lin Ma, "What Does Heidegger Have to Do with an East-West Dialogue?" in *Dao: A Journal of Comparative Philosophy* 4.2 (2005): 312.

30. Saussy, *Great Walls of Discourse,* 32.

31. Tomio Tezuka, "An Hour with Heidegger," in Reinhard May, *Heidegger's Hidden Sources: East Asian Influences on His Work,* trans. Graham Parkes (London: Routledge, 1996), 59–64.

32. Saussy, *Great Walls of Discourse,* 31.

33. Ibid., 113, 160.

34. Edouard Glissant, *Poetics of Relation,* trans. Betsy Wing (Ann Arbor: University of Michigan Press, 1997), 15, 19.

35. Joseph W. Prueher, "The Ambassador's Letter," www.pbs.org/newshour/bb/asia/china/plane/letter_4–11.html (accessed July 22, 2005).

Index